THE PASSIVE INCOME PLAYBOOK:

Building Wealth While You Sleep

BY

CHARLIE DALLANS

CONTENT

<u>**Introduction**</u>

Building wealth while you sleep remains an elusive dream for many in a world marked by the relentless hustle and the perpetual pursuit of success. The clamor of daily life, the demands of a career, and the constant pressure to make ends meet often leave us yearning for a financial escape, a pathway to prosperity that transcends time and effort limitations. Within this desire for financial freedom, "The Passive Income Playbook: Building Wealth While You Sleep" emerges as a beacon of hope and a guide to unlocking the secrets of a lifeless bond by the constraints of traditional wealth-building methods.

In the following pages, we embark on a journey transcending the conventional wisdom surrounding money and success. The Passive Income Playbook is not merely a manual; it is a comprehensive roadmap that navigates the reader through the diverse landscape of passive income streams, each a tributary leading to the river of financial independence. This book is your key to understanding and harnessing the power of passive income – a force that has the potential to reshape your financial destiny.

As we dive into the depths of this playbook, we will explore the multifaceted world of passive income, dissecting its various forms and unveiling the strategies that can turn your dreams of financial autonomy into a tangible reality. From dividend investing and real estate to online businesses and intellectual property, each chapter is a step towards unraveling the mysteries of wealth generation that require less hands-on involvement.

But this isn't just another financial manual. "The Passive Income Playbook" is a call to action, challenging you to rethink your approach to money and wealth. It is a wake-up call for those tethered to the grindstone, urging them to look beyond the limitations of a nine-to-five existence and consider alternative avenues that pave the way to true financial freedom. The time to break free from economic dependency is now, and the Passive Income Playbook is your passport to that liberation.

So, fasten your seatbelt and prepare to embark on a transformative journey. Whether you're a seasoned investor looking to diversify your portfolio or a novice eager to explore uncharted financial territories, this playbook is designed to meet you where you are and guide you to where you want to be. Let the exploration of passive income possibilities begin, for in these pages lies the blueprint for building wealth while you sleep.

What is passive income?

The concept of passive income stands as a beacon of financial freedom. Passive income is not merely a buzzword but a paradigm shift in the traditional understanding of earning a living. In this chapter, we will delve into the depths of passive income, its significance, and how one can harness its power for financial independence.

At its core, passive income refers to earnings derived from ventures or investments that require little to no direct effort from the recipient. Unlike the conventional model of trading time for money, passive income allows individuals to generate revenue with minimal ongoing involvement. This income stream often requires upfront time, energy, or financial investment, but once established, it has the potential to generate returns over an extended period.

Passive income can manifest through various channels, and individuals often diversify their portfolios to create a robust and sustainable financial ecosystem. Here are some familiar sources of passive income:

Dividend Stocks: Investing in dividend-paying stocks allows shareholders to receive regular payouts, typically every quarter.

Real Estate: Rental income from properties is a classic example of passive income, where property owners earn money through tenants.

Business Ownership: Owning a business without constant supervision can generate passive income. This might involve hiring a capable management team or leveraging automated systems.

Royalties: Authors, musicians, and artists can earn passive income through royalties on their creative works.

Affiliate Marketing: Promoting products or services through affiliate links and earning a commission on sales is a popular form of passive income.

Digital Products: Creating and selling digital products like e-books, courses, or software can generate ongoing revenue.

Peer-to-Peer Lending: Lending money through online platforms and earning interest on repayments is a form of passive income.

Certificates of Deposit (CDs): Investing in CDs provides a fixed interest rate over a specified period, generating passive returns.

Passive income liberates individuals from the shackles of a 9-to-5 job, allowing them to pursue personal interests and hobbies.

Diversifying passive income sources mitigates risk, as a downturn in one area may offset gains in another.

Over time, the compounding effect of passive income can lead to substantial wealth accumulation, providing a cushion for unexpected expenses and retirement.

Understanding different passive income streams and investment options is crucial. Continuous learning is the foundation for making informed decisions.

Investing time and resources strategically at the outset is essential. This might involve diligent research, seeking expert advice, and carefully selecting investments aligned with one's financial goals.

Building significant passive income takes time. Consistent effort, even in small increments, can yield substantial results over the long term.
Economic landscapes change, and so should passive income strategies. Being adaptable to market trends and adjusting investment portfolios accordingly is crucial.

Passive income is a powerful tool for achieving financial independence and building lasting wealth. It requires strategic planning, risk management, and a commitment to continuous improvement. As individuals embark on their journey to create passive income streams, they secure their financial future and open the door to a life enriched with opportunities and choices.

Welcome to the World of Passive Income

In finance and entrepreneurship, a magical realm exists known as the "World of Passive Income." It is a place where money works for you, where the effort you put in upfront yields returns long after you've moved on to other endeavors. Welcome, dear reader, to a

journey that promises financial freedom and the luxury of time –
welcome to the world of passive income.

Passive income is the art of making money while you sleep. Unlike
active income, which requires constant time and effort, passive
income allows you to generate earnings with minimal day-to-day
involvement. It's about more than trading time for money; it's about
setting up systems and investments that work on your behalf,
requiring less of your direct attention over time.

The World of Passive Income is diverse, offering many streams
catering to different preferences, risk tolerances, and skill sets.
Among the stars of this realm are:

Investing in dividend-paying stocks allows you to regularly receive
a share of a company's profits. As you accumulate more shares,
your passive income grows.

Owning rental properties or investing in real estate crowdfunding
platforms provides a steady income stream through rent or
property appreciation.

Authors, musicians, and artists benefit from royalties generated by
their creations. This could include books, music, art, or even
patented inventions.

Promoting other people's products and earning a commission on
sales can be a lucrative passive income stream, especially in the
digital age.
 Niche websites, dropshipping, and e-commerce platforms can be
set up to run almost autonomously, generating income through
online sales.

The allure of passive income lies in its promise of financial
freedom. It allows you to break free from the traditional 9-to-5

grind, granting you the flexibility to live on your terms. The goal is to build a portfolio of passive income streams that collectively cover your living expenses and then some, giving you the freedom to pursue your passions and interests without being bound by the constraints of a paycheck.

Embarking on the journey into the World of Passive Income requires knowledge, strategy, and, most importantly, the willingness to take calculated risks. It's not a get-rich-quick scheme but a disciplined approach to wealth-building that pays off over time.

We will delve deeper into each passive income stream, exploring the strategies, challenges, and success stories that define this captivating world. Whether you're a seasoned entrepreneur or just starting to explore financial independence, prepare to unlock the secrets of generating wealth while embracing the freedom to live on your own terms. Welcome to the World of Passive Income – where your money works as hard as you do, if not harder.

Understanding the Power of Passive Wealth

In financial prosperity, passive wealth is a powerful force, often misunderstood and underestimated. This chapter delves into the intricacies of passive wealth, unraveling its potential and the transformative impact it can have on individuals' lives.

Passive wealth refers to the accumulation of financial resources without direct, active involvement in day-to-day income-generating activities, unlike active income, where one exchanges time and effort for money, passive wealth is cultivated through strategic investments, intelligent financial decisions, and the cultivation of assets that generate returns over time.

At the heart of passive wealth lies the art of investing. Investing wisely can pave the way for consistent returns, whether it's stocks, bonds, real estate, or other instruments. Diversifying one's investment portfolio spreads risk and ensures that the impact of market fluctuations is mitigated.

Real estate, a tangible asset, is a cornerstone of passive wealth. Owning properties, renting them out, or engaging in real estate development can yield continuous income streams. The value appreciation of real estate assets further enhances the potential for long-term wealth accumulation.
In the digital age, intellectual property such as books, music, patents, and trademarks can be lucrative passive income sources. Earnings generated from licensing and using intellectual creations can continue over time, providing a steady flow of wealth.

One of the most compelling aspects of passive wealth is the phenomenon of compounding. As returns generate additional returns, the growth of wealth accelerates exponentially. This compounding effect becomes particularly potent over extended periods, emphasizing the importance of a long-term perspective in building passive wealth.

The most enticing aspect of passive wealth is the freedom it affords. Unlike the traditional model of trading time for money, passive wealth liberates individuals from the constraints of a nine-to-five existence. This newfound freedom grants the luxury of time to pursue passions, spend with loved ones, and engage in meaningful experiences beyond the boundaries of a paycheck.

While passive wealth offers numerous advantages, it is not without its risks. Market fluctuations, economic downturns, and poor investment decisions can pose challenges. However, with ongoing education and adaptability, a well-considered and diversified approach can help navigate and mitigate these risks.

Building passive wealth requires more than financial acumen; it demands a mindset shift. Embracing a disciplined approach to savings, staying informed about investment opportunities, and fostering patience are critical components of this mindset. Moreover, understanding the difference between good and bad debt and wisely leveraging assets are crucial to cultivating passive wealth.

The power of passive wealth lies in its financial rewards and ability to transform lives. It is a journey of strategic decisions, calculated risks, and a steadfast commitment to long-term goals. As individuals harness the potential of passive wealth, they find themselves on a path to financial independence, security, and the freedom to design a life rich in experiences and fulfillment.

Chapter 1: The Passive Income Mindset

The concept of passive income has gained significant attention. Many individuals are drawn to generating income with minimal active involvement, allowing them to break free from the traditional 9-to-5 grind and achieve a more flexible and fulfilling lifestyle. This desire for financial autonomy has given rise to what is known as the Passive Income Mindset.

Passive income is the Holy Grail for those seeking financial independence. Unlike active income, which requires ongoing effort and time, passive income streams enable individuals to earn money with less direct involvement. It's not about working harder; it's about working smarter. Passive income can come from various sources, such as investments, real estate, royalties, and online businesses.

Understanding the nature of passive income is crucial. It's not about getting rich overnight but building sustainable revenue streams that continue to flow over time. This mindset shift is fundamental to the journey toward financial freedom.

The Passive Income Mindset challenges the conventional 9-to-5 mentality that has long been the norm. Instead of solely relying on a job for income, individuals with this mindset seek opportunities to create income streams that work for them, even when they're not actively working.

Breaking free from the 9-to-5 mindset requires a shift in perspective. Rather than viewing time as the sole currency for earning money, those embracing the Passive Income Mindset recognize the value of assets, systems, and leverage. Time becomes an ally in building and growing passive income streams.

Central to the Passive Income Mindset is the understanding that assets and leverage play a pivotal role in creating sustainable income. Assets, whether rental properties, dividend-paying stocks, or online courses, can generate income over time without constant attention.

Leverage amplifies the impact of your efforts. Instead of relying solely on your time and skills, you use tools, systems, and other people's expertise to enhance your productivity and efficiency. This strategic use of resources is a critical component of the Passive Income Mindset.

Diversification is a cornerstone of financial success, and it's no different when adopting the Passive Income Mindset. Relying on a single income stream can be risky; therefore, creating a diverse portfolio of passive income sources provides stability and resilience.

A well-rounded portfolio may include stocks, bonds, real estate, online businesses, and intellectual property investments. Each source contributes to the overall financial picture, reducing dependence on any avenue and mitigating risks.

The journey toward passive income is not a sprint but a marathon. Those with a Passive Income Mindset understand the importance of patience and persistence. Building and scaling passive income streams takes time, dedication, and a willingness to learn from failures.

A long-term perspective involves setting realistic expectations and understanding that setbacks are part of the process. Instead of being discouraged by challenges, individuals with a Passive Income Mindset view them as opportunities for growth and improvement.

In a rapidly evolving world, a passive income mindset embraces the idea of lifelong learning. Staying informed about market trends, investment strategies, and emerging opportunities is essential. The ability to adapt to changes and seize new possibilities is a hallmark of the Passive Income Mindset.

From books and courses to networking and mentorship, those with the mindset actively seek knowledge to refine their strategies and stay ahead of the curve. Pursuing education is not a one-time event but an ongoing commitment to personal and financial development.

At its core, the Passive Income Mindset is rooted in the belief that there is an abundance of opportunities in the world. Rather than succumbing to a scarcity mindset, individuals with this mindset recognize that with creativity, resourcefulness, and effort, they can tap into the wealth of possibilities around them.

This shift from scarcity to abundance opens the door to innovation, collaboration, and a positive outlook on the future. It fuels the determination to explore new avenues, take calculated risks, and achieve financial freedom.

Adopting the Passive Income Mindset is not just about making money while you sleep; it's a holistic approach to life and wealth. It involves redefining the relationship with time, embracing the power of assets and leverage, building a diverse portfolio, maintaining a long-term perspective, committing to continuous learning, and cultivating a mindset of abundance. As we delve deeper into the chapters ahead, we will explore practical strategies, case studies, and real-life examples that illuminate the path to a more financially liberated and fulfilling life.

Shifting Your Perspective for Financial Success

One of the most powerful tools in the journey toward financial success is the ability to shift your perspective. How you perceive money, wealth, and success can significantly impact your financial decisions and outcomes. This chapter will explore the transformative power of changing your mindset and adopting a perspective that aligns with economic prosperity.

Your thoughts have a direct influence on your actions, and your actions shape your financial reality. Embracing a positive mindset can be a catalyst for financial success. Start by recognizing and challenging any negative beliefs about money. Replace thoughts of scarcity with thoughts of abundance. Instead of dwelling on economic challenges, focus on potential solutions and opportunities. A positive outlook can open your mind to creative and resourceful ways of managing your finances.

A growth mindset involves seeing challenges as opportunities for learning and growth. Apply this concept to your financial life by viewing setbacks as temporary and surmountable. Understand that your financial situation is not fixed; it can evolve through learning, adaptability, and resilience. Embrace the idea that you can improve your financial literacy, enhance your earning potential, and make informed decisions that lead to prosperity.

Take a moment to reflect on what success means to you. Many people associate success solely with monetary wealth, but proper financial success extends beyond the balance in your bank account. Consider factors such as personal fulfillment, work-life balance, and meaningful relationships. By broadening your definition of success, achieving financial goals becomes more rewarding and sustainable.

Investing in yourself can yield the highest returns. This can include education, skill development, and mental and physical well-being.

Recognize that your greatest asset is your potential. By continuously investing in your growth and well-being, you position yourself for long-term financial success. This perspective shift enhances your earning potential and contributes to a more fulfilling life.

Shift your perspective on spending by adopting a more mindful approach. Before purchasing, consider whether it aligns with your financial goals and values. Cautious spending involves understanding the difference between needs and wants, prioritizing essentials, and avoiding impulse purchases. This conscious approach to spending can lead to increased savings, reduced debt, and a more intentional financial path.

Diversifying your income streams is a strategic perspective shift that can enhance financial stability and success. Explore additional ways to generate income instead of relying solely on a traditional job. This could involve investments, side businesses, or passive income streams. Multiple sources of income provide a safety net and create opportunities for accelerated wealth-building.

Gratitude is a powerful force that can positively impact your financial perspective. Instead of focusing on what you lack, appreciate what you have. Gratitude can foster contentment, reduce the desire for unnecessary spending, and promote financial mindfulness. Recognizing and appreciating your current financial situation sets the stage for
attracting more abundance into your life.

Shifting your perspective for financial success is not just about money; it's about cultivating a mindset that aligns with prosperity in all aspects of life. As you integrate these perspective shifts into your financial journey, remember that change takes time and consistency. Be patient with yourself, stay committed to your goals, and watch as your new mindset transforms your financial reality.

Overcoming Common Mindset Blocks

Our minds are powerful tools that propel us forward or hold us back. How we think our mindset plays a crucial role in shaping our actions and, ultimately, our destinies. However, many individuals face standard mindset blocks that impede personal and professional growth. In this chapter, we'll explore some of these obstacles and, more importantly, discuss practical strategies to overcome them.

One of the fundamental mindset blocks is the division between a fixed mindset and a growth mindset. Those with a fixed mindset believe that abilities and intelligence are innate and unchangeable. In contrast, those with a growth mindset see them as qualities that can be developed through dedication and effort. Overcoming a fixed mindset involves recognizing that challenges and failures are opportunities for learning and growth. Embracing a growth mindset opens doors to continuous improvement and resilience.

The fear of failure is a pervasive mindset block that often prevents individuals from taking risks and pursuing their goals. To overcome this block, reframing failure as a stepping stone to success is essential. Understand that setbacks are not permanent but valuable lessons that contribute to personal development. Cultivating a positive relationship with failure encourages experimentation, innovation, and resilience to navigate life's challenges.

Imposter syndrome is a phenomenon where individuals doubt their accomplishments and fear being exposed as frauds despite evidence of their competence. Overcoming imposter syndrome involves acknowledging achievements, internalizing success, and recognizing that everyone, even the most accomplished individuals, faces self-doubt. Cultivating self-compassion and seeking external validation can help combat imposter syndrome and build confidence.

Some individuals fall into the trap of all-or-nothing thinking, viewing situations in extreme, black-and-white terms. This rigid mindset can hinder progress by creating unnecessary pressure and limiting options. Overcoming this block involves adopting a more nuanced perspective.

Recognize that success is often incremental, and setbacks are not permanent failures. Break down significant goals into smaller, more manageable steps, fostering a more realistic and achievable approach.

In the age of social media, the comparison trap is a standard mindset block. Constantly measuring oneself against others can lead to feelings of inadequacy and hinder personal growth. Overcoming this block requires consciously focusing on individual progress rather than external benchmarks. Celebrate personal achievements, no matter how small, and understand that everyone's journey is unique. Cultivate gratitude for your path and accomplishments.

Sometimes, deeply ingrained beliefs can act as mental roadblocks. Overcoming these requires a willingness to challenge and reassess long-held convictions. Embrace a mindset of curiosity, open-mindedness, and adaptability. Consider alternative perspectives and be open to change. This flexibility in thinking allows for personal and intellectual growth, breaking down the barriers created by rigid beliefs.

Overcoming standard mindset blocks is a continual process of self-reflection, learning, and growth. Individuals can unlock their full potential by cultivating a growth mindset, reframing failure, addressing imposter syndrome, avoiding all-or-nothing thinking, sidestepping the comparison trap, and challenging inflexible beliefs. It's a journey that requires patience, self-compassion, and a commitment to continuous improvement. As we navigate the complex landscape of our minds, let us strive to overcome these mindset blocks and pave the way for a more fulfilling and successful life.

Chapter 2: The Foundation: Setting Financial Goals

The journey toward financial well-being begins with a clear and thoughtful goal-setting process in the vast landscape of personal finance. Articulating and defining one's financial objectives is the cornerstone of a solid financial foundation. This chapter delves into the critical realm of setting financial goals, emphasizing their pivotal role in shaping the trajectory of your financial future.

Financial goals serve as a roadmap for your financial journey, providing direction, purpose, and motivation. Whether your aspirations include homeownership, retirement, education, travel, or debt reduction, each goal represents a unique destination on your financial map. With a clear understanding of these destinations, navigating the complex terrain of personal finance becomes more accessible.

Setting financial goals requires a delicate balance between aspirations and the realities of your current financial situation. It's an exercise in self-reflection, demanding an honest assessment of your income, expenses, assets, and liabilities. This chapter guides you through aligning your dreams with the practicalities of your financial landscape.

Not all financial goals are created equal. Some are immediate and pressing, demanding attention in the short term, while others unfold over years or even decades. This chapter explores the nuances of short-term and long-term financial goals, helping you prioritize and strategize effectively.

To transform your financial dreams into actionable plans, it's essential to employ a structured approach. This chapter introduces the SMART criteria - Specific, Measurable, Achievable, Relevant, and Time-bound - as a framework for crafting inspiring but also practical and attainable goals.

Recognizing that personal finance is inherently subjective, this chapter emphasizes tailoring your financial goals to your unique circumstances, values, and priorities. By understanding your motivations, you can create goals that resonate with your aspirations, enhancing the likelihood of successful implementation.

Achieving financial goals extends beyond mere accomplishment; it has a transformative impact on various facets of your life. This chapter explores the ripple effect of goal achievement, shedding light on how successful financial planning can enhance your overall well-being and bring about positive change.

As we embark on this exploration of setting financial goals, remember that this process is not static. It evolves as your life unfolds, requiring periodic reassessment and adjustment. By laying a solid foundation through thoughtful goal-setting, you empower yourself to navigate the financial landscape with purpose and confidence. Let's embark on this journey together, shaping a future where your economic aspirations become your reality.

Defining Your Financial Freedom

Financial freedom is a concept that goes beyond mere wealth accumulation; it encapsulates the ability to live life on your terms, unburdened by financial constraints. In this chapter, we will explore the nuances of defining your financial freedom, understanding that it's a profoundly personal and evolving journey.

Begin by identifying your core values. What truly matters to you in life? Is it family, adventure, creativity, or something else? Financial freedom should align with these values to ensure a fulfilling and purpose-driven journey.

Define specific, measurable, and realistic financial goals. Whether buying a home, starting a business, or traveling the world, your goals are milestones on your path to financial freedom. Break them down into short-term and long-term objectives.

Conduct a thorough analysis of your current financial status. This includes understanding your income, expenses, assets, and liabilities. Awareness of your economic baseline is crucial for crafting an effective strategy to achieve financial freedom.

Develop a realistic budget that reflects your lifestyle and goals. Categorize your expenses, prioritize essential needs, and allocate funds for savings and investments. A well-structured budget is the foundation for building wealth and attaining financial freedom.

Relying solely on a traditional job may limit your financial growth. Explore additional income streams like investments, freelancing, or a side business. Diversification provides a safety net and accelerates the journey to financial freedom.

Educate yourself on various investment options, including stocks, bonds, real estate, and retirement accounts. Develop an investment strategy aligned with your risk tolerance and financial goals. Consistent, informed investing is a critical element of wealth accumulation.

Prioritize paying off high-interest debts to reduce financial stress and free up resources for wealth-building activities. This includes credit cards, personal loans, and other debts with significant interest rates.
4.2 Controlling Lifestyle Inflation:

As your income increases, resist the temptation to inflate your lifestyle proportionally. Instead, allocate the surplus towards savings and investments. Controlling lifestyle inflation is essential for maintaining a sustainable financial freedom journey.

Financial landscapes evolve, and staying informed is crucial. Continually educate yourself on personal finance, investment strategies, and economic trends. Knowledge empowers you to make informed decisions and adapt your financial plan accordingly.

Recognize that life is unpredictable. Embrace flexibility in your financial plan to accommodate unexpected changes. Being adaptable allows you to navigate challenges without compromising your path to financial freedom.

Defining your financial freedom requires self-awareness, strategic planning, and continuous adaptation. By aligning your values, setting meaningful goals, and adopting sound financial practices, you embark on a journey that transcends monetary wealth, leading to a life rich in purpose and fulfillment.

SMART Goals and Your Path to Passive Income

Passive income is the dream of many aspiring entrepreneurs and investors. The allure of earning money while you sleep or travel the world is undeniably powerful. However, achieving passive income requires more than wishful thinking; it demands strategic planning and a clear roadmap. In this chapter, we'll explore the concept of SMART goals and how they can be your guiding light on the journey to passive income.

SMART is an acronym for Specific, Measurable, Achievable, Relevant, and Time-Bound. This framework is widely used in various fields, including business, project management, and personal development. When applied to the pursuit of passive income, SMART goals provide a structured approach to help you stay focused and motivated.

Define your passive income goal with precision. Instead of a vague desire like "I want to make money online," be specific about the income stream you aim to create. Clarity is critical, whether it's through real estate, investments, or an online business.

I will generate $5,000 monthly in passive income through affiliate marketing within 12 months.

Establish clear metrics to track your progress. With measurable criteria, it's easier to determine whether you're moving in the right direction. Quantify your goals to make them tangible and trackable.

"I will track monthly affiliate sales and aim for a 10% increase each month until reaching $5,000 in monthly passive income."

Ensure that your goal is realistic and attainable. While dreaming big is encouraged, setting impossible goals can lead to frustration and disappointment. Assess your resources, skills, and the market's potential realistically.

Considering my current skills and available time, achieving a 10% monthly increase in affiliate sales is challenging but realistic."

Align your passive income goal with your overall objectives and values. The pursuit of passive income should complement your life, not dominate it. Ensure that your goal is relevant to your long-term vision and aspirations.

Generating passive income through affiliate marketing aligns with my goal of financial freedom and flexibility in my lifestyle."

Set a deadline for achieving your passive income goal. A sense of urgency can propel you into action. Without a timeframe, your goal may lack the motivation to make consistent progress.

I will achieve $5,000 in monthly passive income through affiliate marketing within 12 months."

"I will purchase two rental properties in the next 24 months."

I will generate $1,500 monthly rental income from each property within the first year."

After consulting with a financial advisor, I have determined that I can secure financing and manage the properties effectively."

Real estate aligns with my long-term goal of building wealth and creating a diversified income portfolio."

I will complete the purchase of the first property within the next six months."

I will build a diversified stock portfolio with an average annual return of 8% within the next five years."

I will invest $10,000 initially and contribute $500 monthly to my portfolio."

Based on historical market performance, an 8% annual return is reasonable."

Stock market investments align with my goal of creating a long-term, growing passive income stream."

I will review and rebalance my portfolio annually for the next five years."
I will create and monetize a niche blog, promoting affiliate products in the personal development space."

I aim to achieve $500 in monthly affiliate sales within the first three months and scale to $5,000 per month within the next 12 months."

I have identified a profitable niche and completed a course on effective affiliate marketing strategies."

Running an online business complements my desire for location independence and financial freedom."

I will dedicate at least 15 weekly hours to the blog and track progress
monthly, adjusting strategies as needed."

SMART goals provide a roadmap, but the journey is rarely linear. Regularly monitor your progress and be ready to adjust your strategies based on what's working and what isn't. Flexibility is crucial, whether it's tweaking your investment portfolio, optimizing your online business, or changing your real estate strategy.

Remember, the path to passive income is a marathon, not a sprint. Celebrate small victories, learn from setbacks, and stay committed to your SMART goals. With persistence and a strategic mindset, you'll be inching closer to the financial freedom and lifestyle you aspire to achieve.

Chapter 3: Types of Passive Income Streams

The concept of passive income has emerged as a powerful and transformative force. Unlike traditional active income, where individuals exchange time and effort for money, passive income streams promise to generate revenue with minimal ongoing effort. This financial paradigm shift has captured the imagination of many aspiring entrepreneurs, investors, and individuals seeking financial freedom.

Passive income can be likened to a silent partner working tirelessly in the background, continuously generating earnings while allowing individuals to break free from the constraints of a 9-to-5 job. In this chapter, we will explore the diverse and dynamic world of passive income streams, understanding the various avenues through which individuals can build wealth, achieve financial independence, and create a more flexible and fulfilling lifestyle.

Before delving into the specific types of passive income streams, it is crucial to grasp the fundamental concept of passive income. At its core, passive income is money earned with little or no direct involvement from the recipient. This stands in contrast to active income, where one must actively participate in a task or job to receive compensation.

Passive income can manifest in various forms, from traditional investments and business ventures to modern digital platforms and emerging technologies. The critical characteristic that unites these diverse streams is their ability to generate revenue over time, with diminishing reliance on continuous active effort.

As we explore different types of passive income, it becomes evident that more than one-size-fits-all approach exists. Diversification, a fundamental principle in financial planning, is equally applicable to passive income strategies. Successful individuals often cultivate diverse passive income streams, mitigating risks and optimizing returns.

This category includes stock dividends, interest from bonds, and rental income from real estate. Investments can generate ongoing returns, providing a steady source of passive income over the long term.
Entrepreneurial endeavors, such as starting a business or investing in an existing one, can yield passive income. This might involve hiring competent managers or utilizing automated systems to reduce direct involvement.

Creators of intellectual property, such as authors, musicians, and inventors, can earn passive income through royalties and licensing agreements. Once the work is created, the income continues without requiring continuous effort.

With the rise of the internet, creating and selling digital products, online courses, or participating in affiliate marketing programs has become a famous avenue for passive income.

Beyond rental income, real estate investments can include:
- Crowdfunding platforms.
- Real estate investment trusts (REITs).
- Other innovative approaches allow individuals to benefit from property appreciation and cash flow.

Investing in stocks that pay regular dividends provides a consistent income stream, allowing investors to benefit from the company's success over time.

Platforms facilitating peer-to-peer lending enable individuals to earn interest by lending money directly to others, often with automated systems.

They provide insights into the mechanics, benefits, and potential pitfalls associated with each type of passive income stream. By the end, readers will have a comprehensive understanding of the myriad opportunities available to them and be better equipped to chart their path toward financial independence through the strategic creation of passive income.

Exploring Different Avenues for Passive Wealth

Diversifying our approach and exploring various avenues that align with our financial goals and risk tolerance is crucial. Passive income is the key to financial freedom, allowing us to break free from the traditional 9-to-5 grind and create streams of income that work for us, even while we sleep. This chapter will explore various avenues for generating passive wealth, each offering unique opportunities and challenges.

Real estate has long been a cornerstone of passive wealth generation. Whether it's rental properties, real estate crowdfunding, or Real Estate Investment Trusts (REITs), the potential for passive income is vast. Owning rental properties can provide a steady income stream through monthly rent payments, while REITs offer a way to invest in real estate without the hassle of property management.

Investing in dividend-paying stocks is another avenue for passive income. By owning shares in companies that distribute a portion of their profits to shareholders, investors can enjoy regular dividend payments. Dividend stocks not only provide income but also offer the potential for capital appreciation over time.

The rise of fintech has paved the way for peer-to-peer lending platforms. These platforms connect borrowers with individual lenders, allowing investors to earn interest on loans. While it comes with risks, peer-to-peer lending can be lucrative for generating passive income through interest payments.

For those with expertise in a particular field, creating and selling online courses can be a rewarding source of passive income. Platforms like Udemy and Teachable allow instructors to share their knowledge, reach a global audience, and earn money while they sleep.

Affiliate marketing involves promoting other people's products and earning a commission for every sale made through your referral. This can be done through blogs, social media, or other online channels. Building a successful affiliate marketing business takes time and effort, but once established, it can generate passive income through ongoing commissions.

Automated online businesses, such as dropshipping or print-on-demand ventures, leverage e-commerce platforms and automation tools to minimize the need for hands-on management. While there is an upfront investment of time and resources, these businesses can become largely self-sufficient, providing passive income through online sales.

Creating and owning intellectual property, such as books, music, or art, can lead to passive income through royalties. Authors, musicians, and artists can earn money whenever their work is sold or licensed. This avenue requires talent and creativity but can provide a steady income stream over the long term.

The world of cryptocurrencies has opened up new opportunities for passive income. Staking, yield farming, and decentralized finance (DeFi) platforms offer ways to earn passive income by participating in blockchain networks. However, it's essential to approach cryptocurrency investments cautiously due to their inherent volatility.

Diversifying your passive income streams across different avenues mitigates risk and maximizes your potential for wealth creation. Each avenue has challenges, and success requires careful consideration, planning, and ongoing monitoring. Remember that building passive wealth is a gradual process, and the key is to stay informed, adapt to market changes, and consistently seek new opportunities to expand and optimize your passive income portfolio.

Choosing the Right Streams for You

Choosing the right stream is a pivotal decision that can shape your future. Whether you're a high school student contemplating your next academic step or looking to switch careers, understanding your interests, strengths, and aspirations is crucial in making an informed choice. This chapter will guide you through selecting the most suitable stream for your unique journey.

The first step in choosing the right stream is introspection. Take the time to reflect on your passions, interests, and skills. Consider what activities make you lose track of time and leave you feeling fulfilled. Identify your strengths and weaknesses, both academically and personally. A clear understanding of yourself will guide you in navigating the myriad available streams.

Once you've gained insight into your preferences, delve into the various streams available. Research the academic and professional landscapes associated with each stream. Talk to professionals in different fields, attend career fairs, and explore online resources. Consider taking aptitude tests or career assessments to understand better how your skills align with other streams.

Seek guidance from mentors, teachers, or career advisors. Their experience and knowledge can provide valuable insights into the demands and rewards of different streams. Discuss your goals, interests, and concerns with them, and be open to their suggestions. A mentor can offer a perspective you might not have considered, helping you make a more informed decision.

The world is dynamic, and career landscapes evolve. Research the current trends and future projections for the streams you are considering. Are specific industries booming? Are there emerging technologies that might impact your chosen field? Anticipating future developments can help you select a stream with long-term viability.

Different streams often require distinct educational pathways. Consider the academic qualifications and prerequisites for each stream. Reflect on your academic strengths and preferences. Some streams require a strong foundation in mathematics, while others emphasize creative or analytical skills. Choose a stream that aligns with your intellectual capabilities and goals.

Your chosen stream should align with your lifestyle preferences and work-life balance goals. Some professions demand long hours and extensive travel, while others offer more flexibility. Reflect on your preferred work environment, the level of social interaction you enjoy, and the potential for work-life harmony.

Evaluate the financial aspects of each stream. Consider the costs of education, potential earning prospects, and job stability. While financial gain should not be the sole factor in your decision, choosing a stream that allows for economic sustainability and personal fulfillment is essential.

The modern job market values versatility and adaptability. Choose a stream that offers room for growth, continuous learning, and adaptability to changing circumstances. This approach ensures you remain relevant and resilient in a dynamic professional landscape.

Choosing the right stream is a personal journey that requires careful consideration and self-reflection. It's not just about picking a career; it's about choosing a lifestyle that aligns with your values and aspirations. By taking the time to understand yourself, researching your options, and seeking guidance, you can navigate the river of possibilities and choose a stream that leads to a fulfilling and prosperous future. Remember, your journey is unique, and the right stream is the one that resonates with your true self.

Chapter 4: Investing in Real Estate for Passive Income

Real estate has long been regarded as a wealth creation and financial stability cornerstone. In the investment world, it stands out as a tangible and resilient asset class, offering many opportunities for those seeking to build passive income streams. Real estate's allure lies in its potential for capital appreciation and its capacity to generate consistent, long-term cash flow.

This chapter delves into the intricacies of investing in real estate for passive income, exploring the principles, strategies, and considerations that can empower investors to harness the full potential of this dynamic market. Whether you are a seasoned investor looking to diversify your portfolio or a newcomer seeking a reliable avenue for wealth accumulation, understanding the nuances of real estate investment can be the key to unlocking financial success with minimal ongoing effort.

Before delving into the strategies for generating passive income through real estate, it is crucial to establish a solid understanding of the fundamental principles that underpin successful real estate investing. Unlike more volatile investment options, such as stocks or cryptocurrencies, real estate offers a sense of permanence and stability. It represents physical assets—land, buildings, and structures—that inherently possess intrinsic value.

This chapter will explore the various types of real estate investments, from residential properties to commercial spaces, and elucidate the factors contributing to their potential for passive income generation. Additionally, it will provide insights into the economic and demographic trends that influence real estate markets, enabling investors to make informed decisions and capitalize on emerging opportunities.

Investing in real estate for passive income requires a strategic approach that aligns with individual financial goals and risk tolerance. This chapter will present a range of proven strategies, including rental properties, real estate investment trusts (REITs), and crowdfunding platforms. Each strategy will be examined in detail, outlining its advantages and challenges.

Moreover, the chapter will discuss the critical aspects of property management, emphasizing how effective management practices can significantly impact the level of passivity in real estate investments. From tenant selection to maintenance considerations, understanding the operational aspects of real estate is essential for creating a genuinely hands-free investment experience.

Like any financial endeavor, real estate investment comes with risks. Successful investors recognize the importance of risk mitigation and employ strategies to safeguard their investments. This chapter will explore risk management techniques specific to real estate, providing insights into market fluctuations, financing risks, and potential challenges associated with property ownership.

Furthermore, the chapter will delve into leveraging real estate as a tool for wealth creation. It will discuss how strategic financing and equity-building can amplify returns, creating a pathway to long-term financial prosperity. Through real-life examples and case studies, readers will understand how to navigate the complexities of real estate investment to achieve sustained, passive income.

Investing in real estate for passive income is a journey that requires knowledge, diligence, and a well-defined strategy. This chapter aims to equip readers with the essential insights and practical guidance to embark on this journey confidently. Whether exploring real estate for the first time or seeking to optimize your existing portfolio, the principles outlined in this chapter will serve as a valuable compass, guiding you toward creating a passive income stream that stands the test of time.

Investing in residential rental properties has long been heralded as a cornerstone of building wealth and generating passive income. The allure of steady monthly cash flow, potential tax benefits, and the promise of long-term appreciation make residential rentals attractive for investors seeking financial independence. This chapter will explore the key elements of investing in residential rental properties, providing you with the knowledge and tools to navigate this rewarding but nuanced terrain.

Selecting the right location is paramount in residential real estate. Proximity to amenities, employment centers, schools, and public transportation can significantly influence a property's desirability. A thorough analysis of the local market trends, vacancy rates, and potential for future growth should guide your decision-making process.

Consider the type of property that aligns with your investment goals. Single-family homes, multifamily units, or condominiums each present unique opportunities and challenges. Additionally, assess the property's condition and potential renovation needs. A well-maintained property attracts reliable tenants and can yield a higher return on investment.

The purchase price and financing terms play a pivotal role in determining the profitability of your investment. Conduct a thorough financial analysis, determining the down payment, mortgage interest rates, property taxes, insurance, and potential maintenance costs. Carefully consider your financing options to maximize returns and minimize risks.

Accurate estimation of rental income is essential for projecting cash flow. Analyze rental rates in the area and assess the potential for rent appreciation. On the expense side, account for property management fees, maintenance, property taxes, insurance, and potential vacancies. Building a comprehensive financial model will help you assess the property's viability as a passive income generator.

Decide whether you will manage the property yourself or enlist the services of a professional property management company. While self-management can save costs, it requires time, effort, and hands-on involvement. Professional management offers convenience but comes with associated fees. Carefully weigh the pros and cons based on your investment goals and personal capacity.

Successful property management hinges on securing reliable tenants. Implement a thorough tenant screening process that includes background checks, credit reports, and rental history. Establish clear and comprehensive lease agreements to protect both parties' interests. Cultivating positive tenant relations fosters a stable and harmonious rental environment.

Diversify your real estate portfolio to spread risk. Consider owning properties in different neighborhoods or cities to reduce vulnerability to local market fluctuations. Regularly reassess your portfolio's performance and adjust your strategy based on evolving market conditions.

Stay abreast of local landlord-tenant laws to ensure compliance and minimize legal risks. Obtain comprehensive insurance coverage to protect against unforeseen events, such as property damage or liability claims. A proactive approach to risk management is crucial for sustaining long-term success.

Understand the tax advantages associated with real estate investment. Deductions for mortgage interest, property taxes, and depreciation can significantly impact your overall tax liability. Consult a tax professional to optimize your tax strategy and capitalize on available benefits.

View residential rental properties as a component of your broader financial strategy. Consider how rental income and property appreciation align with your long-term financial goals, such as retirement planning or funding education. Regularly reassess your investment portfolio and adjust your strategy to meet evolving financial objectives.

Investing in residential rental properties for passive income requires a holistic approach encompassing careful property selection, financial analysis, effective property management, risk mitigation, and strategic financial planning. By mastering these elements, you can unlock the full potential of residential real estate as a vehicle for generating consistent and sustainable passive income.

Commercial Real Estate Investments: The Gateway to Passive Income

Investing in commercial real estate (CRE) has long been considered a strategic move for those seeking to generate passive income. Unlike residential real estate, which primarily involves single-family homes or multi-unit dwellings, commercial properties cater to businesses, offering a unique set of opportunities and challenges. This chapter will explore the fundamentals of commercial real estate investments and how they can serve as a lucrative avenue for passive income.

Understanding Commercial Real Estate

Commercial real estate encompasses various property types, including office buildings, retail spaces, industrial warehouses, and multifamily apartment complexes. Each category offers distinct advantages and considerations, depending on the investor's goals and risk tolerance.

One of the primary benefits of commercial real estate is its ability to provide investors with a diversified portfolio. Unlike residential properties, which may be heavily influenced by local economic conditions and housing market fluctuations, commercial properties are often tied to broader economic trends. As a result, commercial real estate investments can offer stability that appeals to those seeking consistent passive income.

The revenue generated from commercial real estate often comes from leasing space to businesses. Lease agreements in the retail sector are typically longer-term and may include provisions for rent increases, providing investors with a predictable income stream. Moreover, tenants in commercial properties often take on additional responsibilities, such as property maintenance and operational costs, reducing the landlord's involvement and increasing the passivity of the investment.

While commercial real estate can offer stability, it has risks. Economic downturns, changes in market demand, and regional economic factors can impact the performance of commercial properties. However, thorough due diligence, careful property selection, and an understanding of market trends can help mitigate these risks.

Investors can choose from various types of commercial real estate, each with its characteristics and potential for passive income.
Suitable for investors seeking stable, long-term tenants, such as professional services or technology firms.

It is attractive for investors interested in properties that cater to retail businesses, with the potential for additional income through profit-sharing or percentage rent.

Ideal for those looking to capitalize on the growing demand for logistics and distribution centers, offering long-term leases and steady income.*
Appealing to investors interested in residential properties on a larger scale, with the potential for consistent rental income.

Strategies for Passive Income in Commercial Real Estate
Shift the burden of property expenses, such as taxes, insurance, and maintenance, to the tenant, maximizing passive income for the investor.

Invest in commercial real estate through publicly-traded REITs, allowing for diversification and liquidity.
Outsource property management to professionals handling day-to-day operations, freeing the investor from active involvement.

Identify properties with potential for improvement or redevelopment, adding value to the asset and increasing passive income over time.

Commercial real estate investments present a compelling opportunity for individuals seeking passive income through real estate. Whether it's the stability of long-term leases, the potential for value appreciation, or the variety of property types to choose from, commercial real estate offers a diverse range of strategies to meet different investment objectives. As with any investment, thorough research, a clear understanding of market dynamics, and a well-defined strategy are essential for success in commercial real estate. By carefully navigating this landscape, investors can unlock the doors to a steady stream of passive income and long-term financial growth.

Real estate crowdfunding is an innovative way for individuals to invest in real estate projects without buying properties outright. It allows investors to pool their resources and collectively invest in various real estate opportunities. This model has gained popularity to generate passive income and diversify investment portfolios. Here are some key points to consider when it comes to real estate crowdfunding for passive income:

Real estate crowdfunding provides investors with the opportunity to diversify their investment portfolios. By participating in various projects across different locations and types of properties, investors can spread risk and potentially enhance returns.

Crowdfunding lowers the entry barriers for real estate investment. Investors can get started with smaller amounts of capital, making it accessible to a broader range of individuals who may not have the resources to purchase entire properties.

Real estate crowdfunding can generate passive income through various structures, such as rental income or profit-sharing from property sales. Investors typically receive returns in proportion to their investment without actively managing properties.

Crowdfunding platforms often involve professional real estate developers or managers who oversee the projects. This allows investors to benefit from the expertise of experienced professionals without having to manage the properties themselves actively.

Crowdfunding platforms leverage technology to streamline the investment process. Investors can browse and select projects online, track their investments, and receive updates through the platform. This makes real estate crowdfunding a convenient and accessible investment option.

There are different models of real estate crowdfunding, including equity crowdfunding and debt crowdfunding. In equity crowdfunding, investors become partial property owners and share in the potential profits. In debt crowdfunding, investors act as lenders, earning interest on the loans provided for real estate projects.

While real estate crowdfunding offers opportunities, it comes with risks. Investors should conduct thorough due diligence on the crowdfunding platform and the specific projects. Market conditions, the project sponsors' track record, and the investment terms should be carefully evaluated.

Real estate investments, including those made through crowdfunding, are generally less liquid than stocks or bonds. Investors should be prepared for their capital to be tied up for the duration of the investment, which may range from several months to several years.

Real estate crowdfunding is subject to regulatory oversight, and platforms must comply with securities laws. Investors should be aware of the regulatory framework governing crowdfunding in their jurisdiction and choose platforms that adhere to these regulations.

Investors should be mindful of the tax implications associated with real estate crowdfunding. Returns may be subject to income or capital gains tax, depending on the investment structure and local tax laws.

Before venturing into real estate crowdfunding, investors must understand their risk tolerance, conduct thorough research, and consider consulting with financial or investment advisors. Each crowdfunding platform and investment opportunity has its own set of terms, conditions, and potential risks, so due diligence is paramount.

Real estate investment has proven to be a lucrative avenue for generating passive income, and one of the most dynamic strategies within this realm is fixed and flip. This strategy involves purchasing distressed properties, renovating them, and selling them at a higher price. While fix and flip is traditionally associated with active real estate investment, savvy investors have found ways to make it a passive income generator. This chapter will delve into the nuances of fix and flip strategies tailored for those seeking passive income.

The key to success in fix and flip lies in identifying properties with the potential for significant appreciation. Passive investors often rely on experienced real estate professionals, such as agents or property managers, to source potential deals. These professionals can leverage their expertise to analyze market trends, property values, and potential renovation costs, allowing passive investors to make informed decisions without hands-on involvement.

Creating a reliable team is crucial for passively executing a fix-and-flip strategy. This team may include contractors, architects, project managers, and real estate agents. Passive investors can hire a project manager or property manager to oversee the entire process, ensuring that renovations stay on schedule and within budget. Building a solid team minimizes the need for direct involvement, making fix and flip a more passive venture.

Passive investors can leverage technology to conduct comprehensive market analyses. Real estate investment platforms and data analytics tools provide valuable insights into market trends, property values, and potential return on investment. By staying informed through these tools, passive investors can make strategic decisions without needing hands-on property visits.

For a genuinely hands-off approach, investors can explore turnkey solutions. Turnkey providers identify, renovate, and manage properties on behalf of investors, offering a fully managed investment experience. While the returns may be slightly lower due to management fees, the convenience of not being involved in the day-to-day operations can be an attractive proposition for passive investors.

Passive investors in fix and flip must prioritize risk management and due diligence. This involves thoroughly vetting potential properties and assessing the associated risks. Passive investors can mitigate the inherent dangers of fix-and-flip investing by relying on experienced professionals and leveraging comprehensive due diligence processes.
Passive investors must have a clear exit strategy to maximize profits.

This involves strategic timing in the selling process to capitalize on market upswings. Real estate professionals can assist in timing the sale for optimal returns, ensuring that passive investors reap the rewards of their investment without actively participating in the selling process.

Fix and flip strategies can be adapted for passive income generation in real estate. By employing a combination of market analysis tools, building a reliable team, and leveraging turnkey solutions, investors can enjoy the benefits of real estate appreciation without the hands-on involvement typically associated with fix and flip. With careful planning, risk management, and strategic decision-making, fix and flip can become a powerful avenue for passive income in real estate investing.

As we delve deeper into real estate investing for passive income, one avenue that deserves special attention is Real Estate Investment Trusts (REITs). REITs offer a unique way for investors to participate in the real estate market without directly owning physical properties. In this chapter, we'll explore the fundamentals of REITs, their benefits, potential risks, and how they fit into a comprehensive strategy for generating passive income through real estate.

Real Estate Investment Trusts are companies that own, operate, or finance income-generating real estate in various sectors such as residential, commercial, or industrial. REITs allow individual investors to access a diversified portfolio of real estate assets without the challenges associated with property management or significant capital requirements.

By law, REITs must distribute at least 90% of their taxable income to shareholders as dividends. This consistent income stream can be a reliable source of passive income for investors.

REITs often own and manage various properties across different sectors and geographical locations. This diversification helps reduce risk by spreading exposure across various real estate markets.

Unlike direct real estate investments, which can be illiquid and require significant time to buy or sell, REITs are traded on stock exchanges. This provides investors with the flexibility to buy or sell shares quickly.

REITs are managed by experienced professionals who handle property management, maintenance, and other operational aspects. This allows investors to enjoy the benefits of real estate ownership without the day-to-day responsibilities.

Investing in REITs is accessible to a broad range of investors. With a relatively low investment threshold, individuals can participate in the real estate market alongside institutional investors.
Potential Risks:

Broader economic conditions, interest rates, and market sentiment can influence REITs. Economic downturns or rising interest rates may impact the performance of the underlying real estate assets.

Since REITs often rely on debt for financing, changes in interest rates can affect their profitability. Rising interest rates can increase borrowing costs, potentially impacting the overall returns.

The success of a REIT is closely tied to the competence of its management team. Investors should carefully evaluate the track record and expertise of the management before investing.

Include REITs as part of a diversified investment portfolio. This can help balance risk and enhance the stability of your overall investment strategy.

Before investing in a REIT, conduct thorough research on its portfolio, management team, historical performance, and dividend history. Look for REITs that align with your risk tolerance and investment objectives.

While REITs can provide regular income, they also benefit from long-term appreciation. Consider holding onto your REIT investments for an extended period to capture income and potential capital gains.

Real Estate Investment Trusts offer a compelling option for investors seeking passive income through real estate. By combining the benefits of consistent dividends, professional management, and liquidity, REITs can play a crucial role in a well-rounded investment strategy. As with any investment, careful consideration, research, and ongoing monitoring are essential to optimize the potential for passive income while managing associated risks.

In the vast landscape of investment opportunities, few avenues, like real estate, offer the potential for wealth creation and stability. Whether you're a seasoned investor or a newcomer to the world of financial planning, understanding the real estate advantage can significantly shape your portfolio and financial future.

Real estate is inherently valuable. Unlike stocks or bonds, which derive value from external factors like market sentiment or interest rates, real estate possesses intrinsic worth. Land and its structures serve fundamental human needs, providing shelter, workspace, and resources. This tangible quality forms a solid foundation for long-term value and stability.

One of the primary advantages of real estate investment is the potential for property appreciation. Over time, well-chosen properties tend to increase in value, reflecting not only the property's improvements but also the overall growth and development of the surrounding area. This appreciation, often outpacing inflation, can significantly enhance your overall wealth.

Real estate serves as a powerful tool for diversifying your investment portfolio. You can reduce risk by including real estate assets by spreading your investments across different asset classes. Real estate markets often behave independently of stock and bond markets, providing a hedge against market volatility. This diversification is crucial during economic downturns when real estate may remain relatively stable while other assets experience fluctuations.

Investing in rental properties offers a consistent income stream through rental payments. This reliable cash flow can provide financial stability, especially in retirement. Well-maintained and strategically located rental properties can yield a steady income while offering the potential for property value appreciation over time.

Real estate investors benefit from various tax advantages. Interest on mortgages, property taxes, operating expenses, and depreciation are deductible expenses that can reduce taxable income. Also, profits from selling certain real estate types may qualify for favorable capital gains treatment. Savvy investors leverage these tax incentives to enhance their overall returns.

Real estate has historically been an effective hedge against inflation. As the cost of living rises, so does the value of real estate. Rental income and property values tend to increase with inflation, helping investors maintain purchasing power and wealth preservation.

Investing in real estate provides control and flexibility that other investments may lack. Investors can improve and manage their properties, implementing strategies to increase their value. This hands-on approach allows for a proactive response to market conditions and economic trends.

Real estate investment provides an opportunity to build a lasting legacy and facilitate wealth transfer across generations. Tangible assets like properties can be passed down to heirs, providing them with a stable financial foundation and potential income streams.

The real estate advantage is a multifaceted and powerful force in the investment world. Its ability to generate consistent income, appreciate value, and offer tax advantages make it a cornerstone for building and preserving wealth. While, like any investment, it comes with risks, a well-informed and strategic approach to real estate can yield substantial long-term rewards, making it an essential component of a diversified and robust investment portfolio.

The Real Estate Advantage

In the vast landscape of investment opportunities, few avenues like real estate offer the potential for wealth creation and stability. Whether you're a seasoned investor or a newcomer to the world of financial planning, understanding the real estate advantage can significantly shape your portfolio and financial future.

Real estate is inherently valuable. Unlike stocks or bonds, which derive value from external factors like market sentiment or interest rates, real estate possesses intrinsic worth. Land and its structures serve fundamental human needs, providing shelter, workspace, and resources. This tangible quality forms a solid foundation for long-term value and stability.

One of the primary advantages of real estate investment is the potential for property appreciation. Over time, well-chosen properties tend to increase in value, reflecting not only the property's improvements but also the overall growth and development of the surrounding area. This appreciation, often outpacing inflation, can significantly enhance your overall wealth.

Real estate serves as a powerful tool for diversifying your investment portfolio. You can reduce risk by including real estate assets by spreading your investments across different asset classes. Real estate markets often behave independently of stock and bond markets, providing a hedge against market volatility. This diversification is crucial during economic downturns when real estate may remain relatively stable while other assets experience fluctuations.

Investing in rental properties offers a consistent income stream through rental payments. This reliable cash flow can provide financial stability, especially in retirement. Well-maintained and strategically located rental properties can yield a steady income while offering the potential for property value appreciation over time.

Real estate investors benefit from various tax advantages. Interest on mortgages, property taxes, operating expenses, and depreciation are deductible expenses that can reduce taxable income. Also, profits from selling certain real estate types may qualify for favorable capital gains treatment. Savvy investors leverage these tax incentives to enhance their overall returns.

Real estate has historically been an effective hedge against inflation. As the cost of living rises, so does the value of real estate. Rental income and property values tend to increase with inflation, helping investors maintain purchasing power and wealth preservation.
Investing in real estate provides control and flexibility that other investments may lack. Investors can improve and manage their properties, implementing strategies to increase their value. This hands-on approach allows for a proactive response to market conditions and economic trends.

Real estate investment provides an opportunity to build a lasting legacy and facilitate wealth transfer across generations. Tangible assets like properties can be passed down to heirs, providing them with a stable financial foundation and potential income streams.

The real estate advantage is a multifaceted and powerful force in the investment world. Its ability to generate consistent income, appreciate value, and offer tax advantages make it a cornerstone for building and preserving wealth. While, like any investment, it comes with risks, a well-informed and strategic approach to real estate can yield substantial long-term rewards, making it an essential component of a diversified and robust investment portfolio.

Strategies for Successful Real Estate Investments

Real estate investment can be lucrative but requires careful planning, market understanding, and strategic decision-making. In this chapter, we will explore various strategies that can contribute to the success of your real estate investments.

Before delving into real estate, defining your investment goals is crucial. Are you looking for long-term appreciation, steady rental income, or a combination? Understanding your objectives will help shape your investment strategy.

Successful real estate investors stay informed about local and national market trends—research factors like job growth, population demographics, and economic indicators. Examine your target area's supply and demand dynamics to identify emerging opportunities.

Diversifying your real estate portfolio can mitigate risks. Consider investing in different properties, such as residential, commercial, or industrial. Geographic diversification can also be beneficial, reducing the impact of localized market fluctuations.

Positive cash flow is vital for sustaining real estate investments. Carefully analyze potential rental income, operating expenses, and mortgage payments. Ensure your property generates enough income to cover all costs and leave room for unexpected expenses.

Using leverage, such as mortgages, can amplify returns and increase risk. Be cautious and evaluate your risk tolerance. Ensure that your cash flow can cover debt service and that you have contingency plans in case of market downturns.

Interest rates, loan terms, and financing options can significantly impact your returns. Stay informed about current lending conditions and explore various financing options to find the most favorable terms for your investment.

Networking is a powerful tool in real estate. Establish connections with real estate professionals, other investors, and industry experts. Attend local events, join real estate investment groups, and actively seek opportunities to learn and collaborate.

Real estate is generally a long-term investment. Adopting a patient and strategic approach can lead to substantial returns over time. Resist the temptation to make impulsive decisions based on short-term market fluctuations.

Consider properties that have the potential for improvement or renovation. Value-added strategies, such as upgrading kitchens and bathrooms or enhancing curb appeal, can increase property value and rental income.

Real estate investments inherently involve risk. Assess and manage risk by conducting due diligence, having adequate insurance coverage, and maintaining a financial buffer for unforeseen circumstances.
The real estate market is dynamic and ever-changing. Stay informed about industry trends, regulations, and emerging technologies. Continuous learning will empower you to make informed decisions and adapt to evolving market conditions.

Successful real estate investment requires careful planning, ongoing education, and strategic execution. By defining clear goals, staying informed, and adopting a patient, long-term perspective, investors can position themselves for success in the dynamic world of real estate.

Chapter 5: Building Passive Income Through Investments

Building passive income through investments is a crucial and decisive strategy. While active income requires direct involvement and effort, passive income allows you to earn money with less active participation. Investing wisely can create streams of income that require minimal day-to-day management, providing you with the financial freedom to pursue your passions and live life on your terms.

Passive income is money earned with little to no ongoing effort. Unlike a regular job where you exchange time for money, passive income sources generate cash flow without requiring constant attention. Investments are one of the most effective ways to build a sustainable and growing passive income stream.

Dividend Stocks: Invest in companies that pay regular dividends. As a shareholder, you receive a portion of the company's profits through dividends.

  - Index Funds: Diversify your portfolio by investing in index funds,
which track the performance of a market index. These funds often pay dividends.

Rental Properties: Owning residential or commercial real estate and renting it out can provide a steady stream of passive income.

  - Real Estate Investment Trusts (REITs): These are investment vehicles that allow you to invest in real estate without directly owning properties. REITs often distribute a significant portion of their income to shareholders.

Platforms like Prosper or LendingClub allow you to lend money directly to individuals, earning interest on the loans.

Start-ups or Small Businesses: Investing in businesses through direct ownership or as a silent partner can yield returns if the business succeeds.

Focus on companies with a history of consistently increasing their dividends. Over time, this strategy can lead to a substantial and growing passive income stream.

Diversifying your investment portfolio is crucial for managing risk. Different asset classes and investment vehicles react differently to market conditions. A well-diversified portfolio can help mitigate the impact of market fluctuations and economic downturns, ensuring a more stable and resilient source of passive income.

While the goal is to generate passive income, it's important to remember that all investments carry some risk. Conduct thorough research before making investment decisions and consider seeking advice from financial professionals. Understand the risks associated with each investment type and develop a strategy that aligns with your financial goals and risk tolerance.

One of the most significant advantages of building passive income through investments is the power of compounding. Reinvesting earnings allows your investments to grow exponentially over time. As your investment grows, so does your passive income, creating a self-sustaining cycle of wealth accumulation.

While passive income requires less day-to-day management, reviewing and adjusting your investment strategy periodically is essential. Market conditions, economic factors, and individual investment performance can change, necessitating adjustments to align your portfolio with your financial goals.

Building passive income through investments is vital to a comprehensive financial strategy. Whether you choose stocks, real estate, or other investment vehicles, the goal is to create a reliable and growing stream of income that allows you to achieve financial freedom. With careful planning, diversification, and a long-term perspective, you can embark on a journey toward financial independence and enjoy the benefits of passive income for years to come.

Understanding Stocks, Bonds, and Mutual Funds

Investing is a critical component of building wealth and achieving financial goals. This chapter will delve into three primary investment instruments: stocks, bonds, and mutual funds. Each plays a distinct role in a diversified investment portfolio and has its characteristics, risks, and potential rewards.

At its core, a stock represents ownership in a company. When you buy shares of a company's stock, you become a partial owner and, as such, have a claim on its assets and earnings. Stocks are traded on the New York Stock Exchange (NYSE) or the NASDAQ.

These give shareholders voting rights in the company and a share in its profits through dividends.

These shareholders have priority over common stockholders in receiving dividends and assets in the event of liquidation.

Stocks have the potential for high returns, capital appreciation, and dividend income.

They are subject to market volatility, and the value of stocks can fluctuate significantly. Company-specific risks, such as poor management decisions or changes in industry conditions, also exist.

Unlike stocks, bonds represent debt. When you buy a bond, you lend money to an entity, such as a government or corporation, in exchange for periodic interest payments and the return of the principal amount at maturity.

Governments issue them to fund public projects. Examples include Treasury bonds and municipal bonds.

Companies issue them to raise capital for various purposes.

Bonds provide fixed interest payments, making them attractive for income-oriented investors. They are generally considered less risky than stocks.

Interest rate changes, credit risk, and inflation can influence bond prices. In some cases, the issuer may default on payments.

A mutual fund pools money from multiple investors to invest in a diversified portfolio of stocks, bonds, or other securities. Professional fund managers make investment decisions on behalf of the investors.
Invest primarily in stocks.

Mutual funds provide instant diversification, professional management, and liquidity. They are suitable for investors with various risk tolerances.
Fund performance can be impacted by management fees, market conditions, and the fund manager's decisions.

Diversifying across different asset classes, such as stocks, bonds, and mutual funds, helps manage risk and optimize returns. A well-balanced portfolio aligns with an investor's financial goals and risk tolerance.

Regularly reviewing your portfolio and making adjustments as needed is crucial. Market conditions, economic factors, and personal circumstances can change, impacting the suitability of your investments.

Understanding stocks, bonds, and mutual funds is fundamental to making informed investment decisions. Each instrument has its unique characteristics and fits different investment objectives. By carefully considering your financial goals, risk tolerance, and time horizon, you can construct a diversified portfolio that aligns with your needs and objectives. Always remember that investing involves risks, and seeking advice from financial professionals can help navigate the complexities of the financial markets.

Creating a Diverse Investment Portfolio

Successful investing is not just about picking the right stocks or timing the market; it's also about constructing a well-balanced and diverse portfolio. Diversification is a critical strategy that can help manage risk and enhance long-term returns. This chapter will explore the importance of diversity in your investment portfolio and provide practical steps to create and maintain a diverse and resilient investment strategy.

Diversification is grounded in the principle of the risk-return tradeoff. By spreading your investments across different asset classes, industries, and geographic regions, you can reduce the overall risk of your portfolio without sacrificing returns. Understanding this tradeoff is fundamental to appreciating the benefits of diversification.

Diversification extends beyond merely investing in different stocks. It involves allocating your investments across various asset classes, such as equities, fixed income, real estate, and commodities. Each asset class has its own risk and return characteristics, and a well-diversified portfolio combines these to achieve a balance that aligns with your financial goals and risk tolerance.

Before constructing your portfolio, assessing your risk tolerance and financial goals is crucial. Are you investing for long-term growth, income, or both? Understanding your objectives will guide the allocation of assets in your portfolio.

Strategic asset allocation involves setting target percentages for different asset classes based on your investment goals. Tactical asset allocation, on the other hand, allows for adjustments based on market conditions. Striking the right balance between these approaches is essential for maintaining a diversified portfolio over time.

Geographic and industry diversification ensures that your portfolio is adequately exposed to the economic conditions of a single country or sector. Consider investing in domestic and international markets and across industries with low correlation.

Over time, market fluctuations can cause your portfolio to deviate from its original asset allocation. Regularly rebalancing your portfolio involves buying and selling assets to align with your intended allocation. This disciplined approach ensures that you are consistently buying low and selling high.

Markets are dynamic, and economic conditions can shift. Stay informed about global events, economic indicators, and market trends. Adjust your portfolio to capitalize on opportunities or protect against emerging risks.

A diverse portfolio is not a one-time creation but requires ongoing attention and adjustment.

These investment vehicles offer instant diversification by pooling money from multiple investors to invest in a diversified portfolio of stocks, bonds, or other assets. ETFs and mutual funds provide easy access to various asset classes and sectors.

Robo-advisors use algorithms to create and manage a diversified portfolio based on your risk tolerance and investment goals. These platforms provide a hands-off approach to diversification, making it accessible to investors with varying levels of expertise.

Creating and maintaining a diverse investment portfolio is a continuous process that evolves with your financial goals, market conditions, and risk tolerance. By embracing diversification, you position yourself to weather market uncertainties and increase the likelihood of achieving long-term financial success. Stay disciplined, stay informed, and let the power of diversity work in your favor as you navigate the exciting world of investing.

Chapter 6: Creating and Selling Digital Products

In the ever-evolving landscape of the digital age, creating and selling digital products has become a lucrative and accessible avenue for entrepreneurs and creatives alike. Whether you're a seasoned professional or a budding enthusiast, the possibilities are vast, and the barriers to entry are lower than ever. This chapter will explore the steps in conceiving, producing, and successfully selling digital products.

Before diving into the creation process, it's essential to identify and understand your target audience. What are their needs, pain points, and desires? Conduct market research, engage with your community, and gather insights to inform your product creation.

Select a niche that aligns with your expertise and resonates with your audience. A focused approach allows you to become a go-to authority in that space and increases the chances of success.

Generate ideas for your digital product and validate them. Use surveys, social media polls, or discussions with your audience to refine your concepts. Ensure there's a demand for what you plan to create.

Create a detailed plan and outline for your digital product. This includes defining the scope, setting milestones, and establishing a timeline. Having a clear roadmap ensures a smoother development process.
Depending on your product type, this could involve writing, designing, coding, or recording. Maintain a high standard of quality, as this will directly impact the perceived value of your digital product.

Before the official launch, create prototypes or beta versions of your digital product. Test them with a select group of users to gather feedback and make necessary improvements.

Select a platform that aligns with your product and target audience. Choose wisely based on your goals, whether it's an e-commerce website, a dedicated platform (e.g., Etsy, Gumroad), or a marketplace (e.g., Amazon, Udemy).

Determine the pricing strategy for your digital product. Consider factors such as production costs, perceived value, and competitive analysis. Experiment with pricing models (e.g., one-time purchase, subscription, freemium) to find the best.

Develop a comprehensive marketing plan to promote your digital product. Leverage social media, email marketing, content marketing, and other channels to generate awareness and build anticipation.

Integrate a secure and user-friendly payment processing system. Options like PayPal, Stripe, or other dedicated e-commerce solutions ensure smooth transactions and build trust with your customers.

Establish a system for customer support to address inquiries, feedback, and issues promptly. Positive customer experiences can lead to repeat business and positive word-of-mouth marketing.

Monitor key metrics such as sales, customer behavior, and feedback. Use analytics tools to gain insights into your product's performance and iterate based on the data gathered.

Understand the legal aspects of creating and selling digital products. Protect your intellectual property by considering copyright laws and licensing agreements.

Ensure that your product complies with data protection regulations. Implement secure practices to safeguard customer information and maintain trust.

As your digital product gains traction, be prepared to scale your operations. This may involve automating specific processes, expanding your team, or optimizing workflows.

Explore opportunities to diversify your product line. This could involve creating complementary products, expanding into different niches, or offering variations of your existing product to cater to a broader audience.

Creating and selling digital products is a dynamic journey that requires a combination of creativity, strategy, and adaptability. You can build a successful digital product business by understanding your audience, delivering value, and staying attuned to market trends. Embrace the learning curve, stay innovative, and enjoy the process of bringing your digital creations to the world.

The World of E-books, Courses, and Apps

In the ever-evolving landscape of digital content, e-book publishing has undergone a transformative journey. As technology advances and consumer preferences shift, the industry is witnessing dynamic trends shaping how authors, publishers, and readers interact with digital literature. This chapter explores the evolving trends in e-book publishing,
focusing on the intersection of online courses and mobile applications.

Traditional e-books have been static digital replicas of print books, but a new era is dawning with the rise of interactive e-books.

These dynamic digital publications go beyond the limitations of their printed counterparts, integrating multimedia elements such as audio, video, and interactive graphics. Authors and publishers leverage these features to create immersive reading experiences, appealing to a tech-savvy audience that craves more than just plain text.

As the demand for online education grows, e-books are becoming integral components of digital courses. Publishers are collaborating with educators to develop e-books that seamlessly integrate with course content, providing students with a multimedia-rich learning experience. These e-books often include embedded quizzes, interactive exercises, and links to supplementary materials, enhancing learners' educational value and engagement.

In the realm of digital education, adaptive learning technology is gaining prominence. E-books are evolving to cater to individual learning styles and preferences, offering personalized learning experiences. Through data analytics and artificial intelligence, e-books can adapt content presentation, difficulty levels, and learning paths based on the user's performance and feedback, fostering a more effective and tailored learning journey.

With the widespread use of smartphones and tablets, mobile learning apps transform how people consume educational content. E-books are no longer confined to dedicated e-reader devices; they are integrated into multifunctional apps that provide a seamless reading and learning experience. These apps often include features such as offline access, note-taking capabilities, and social sharing, making learning on the go more accessible and interactive.

Social media and online communities connect authors directly with their readers. E-books are now being released with built-in forums, discussion boards, or author Q&A sessions, fostering a sense of community and interaction. This trend enhances the reader's experience and gives authors valuable feedback and insights, influencing their future works.

The subscription-based model is reshaping how readers access e-books. Platforms like Kindle Unlimited, Audible, and Scribd offer subscribers unlimited access to a vast library of e-books, audiobooks, and other digital content. This shift towards subscription services provides readers with cost-effective and diverse options while challenging traditional publishing models.

As technology advances, e-books explore the realms of augmented and virtual reality. Enhanced by AR and VR, e-books can transport readers into immersive environments, bringing narratives to life in unimaginable ways. This trend caters to entertainment and holds immense potential for educational content, providing interactive and experiential learning opportunities.

The world of e-books is undergoing a profound transformation, influenced by technological advancements, changing consumer behaviors, and the demand for innovative educational solutions.

Integrating e-books with online courses and mobile applications creates a dynamic ecosystem that extends beyond traditional publishing boundaries, opening up new possibilities for authors, publishers, educators, and readers alike. As we navigate this evolving landscape, one thing is sure: the future of e-book publishing is exciting and full of potential.

A seismic shift was underway in the fast-evolving landscape of education as traditional learning paradigms gave way to the rise of online learning platforms. The intersection of e-books, courses, and apps marked a transformative era, reshaping how knowledge was acquired and disseminated.

The digital renaissance dawned upon the educational landscape with the advent of online learning platforms. Once confined to static PDFs, E-books transformed into dynamic, interactive formats, blurring the lines between traditional textbooks and digital resources. This transition not only enhanced accessibility but also laid the groundwork for the integration of multimedia elements, making learning a more immersive experience.

Many online learning platforms emerged, catering to diverse learning styles and subjects. From specialized platforms focused on coding, language learning, and creative arts to comprehensive platforms offering a spectrum of courses, learners were spoiled for choice. The competition sparked innovation, with platforms constantly refining their offerings to stay relevant in a rapidly changing landscape.

As e-books evolved, they seamlessly integrated with online courses. Learners could now access supplementary reading materials, interactive quizzes, and multimedia content directly within the e-book interface. This convergence blurred the lines between traditional textbooks and course materials, creating a unified and cohesive learning experience.

Learning apps, designed for both mobile devices and desktops, became indispensable tools in the educational arsenal. These apps offered bite-sized lessons, quizzes, and interactive activities, allowing learners to engage with course content on the go. Gamification elements, such as badges and rewards, added a layer of motivation, turning education into a more enjoyable and rewarding endeavor.

One of the defining features of online learning platforms was the ability to tailor education to individual needs. Machine learning algorithms analyzed user data, tracking progress and identifying areas of improvement. With this information, platforms could recommend personalized learning paths, ensuring that each learner's journey is unique and optimized for their success.

The rise of online learning platforms shattered geographical barriers, providing learners worldwide access to high-quality education. Students in remote corners of the globe could now enroll in courses from prestigious institutions, interact with educators, and collaborate with peers from diverse cultural backgrounds. The democratization of education was in full swing, empowering learners regardless of their location.

Despite the myriad benefits, the rise of online learning platforms posed its own set of challenges. Issues such as digital inequality, the need for digital literacy, and concerns about the quality of online education became hot topics of discussion. However, these challenges also presented opportunities for innovation, collaboration, and the development of solutions to bridge the gaps.

As the digital landscape continued to evolve, the future of online learning platforms hinted at even greater integration. Augmented reality (AR) and virtual reality (VR) technologies were poised to revolutionize the learning experience, creating immersive environments that transported learners to virtual classrooms, historical events, or scientific experiments.

This chapter witnessed the transformative power of online learning platforms in The World of E-books, Courses, and Apps. The convergence of e-books, courses, and apps redefined how we access information and paved the way for a more inclusive, personalized, and globally connected education system. The journey had just begun, and the future promised a seamless integration of technology and learning, unlocking new possibilities for the curious minds of tomorrow.

As technology continues to advance at an unprecedented pace, the world of education has undergone a remarkable transformation. Traditional teaching methods gradually give way to innovative educational apps, creating a dynamic and engaging learning environment for students of all ages. This chapter explores the cutting-edge innovations in e-books, courses, and educational apps that reshape the learning landscape.

The evolution of e-books has transcended static digital pages. Interactive e-books now feature multimedia elements such as videos, quizzes, and simulations, enhancing the learning experience. These immersive tools give students a more dynamic way to engage with educational content, fostering deeper comprehension and retention.

E-books have evolved to incorporate adaptive learning algorithms, tailoring content based on individual student progress and learning styles. Personalized learning paths ensure that each student receives a customized educational experience, addressing their strengths and weaknesses.

Facilitating collaboration in the virtual space, collaborative e-books enable students and educators to work together in real time. This fosters a sense of community and allows for collective knowledge creation, transforming the learning process into a collaborative and interactive endeavor.

Innovative online courses have embraced gamification to make learning more engaging and enjoyable. By integrating game elements such as points, badges, and leaderboards, students are motivated to progress and achieve learning objectives, turning education into a rewarding and interactive experience.

The emergence of virtual reality has revolutionized online courses, offering immersive experiences that transport students to different environments. VR courses provide a hands-on, practical approach to learning, particularly in fields like science, medicine, and engineering, where experiential learning is crucial.

Recognizing the value of time and attention, online courses have adopted microlearning modules—bite-sized lessons that can be consumed quickly. This approach accommodates busy schedules and enhances information retention, catering to the needs of learners in the fast-paced digital age.

AI-powered tutoring apps have revolutionized the one-on-one learning experience. These apps use machine learning algorithms to understand the unique learning patterns of each student, providing targeted feedback and personalized assistance, effectively acting as virtual tutors available 24/7.

Augmented reality apps overlay digital information onto the physical world, creating an interactive and immersive learning experience. AR learning apps bring subjects like history, geography, and anatomy to life, allowing students to explore and interact with 3D models and simulations.

Educational apps now emphasize social interaction, creating virtual communities where students can connect, collaborate, and share knowledge. Social learning platforms foster a sense of belonging and enable peer-to-peer support, enhancing the learning experience.

The innovations in educational apps within the world of e-books, courses, and apps are redefining the future of learning. As technology advances, educators and developers are pushing the boundaries of what is possible, creating a more inclusive, personalized, and engaging educational landscape for learners worldwide. The education journey is evolving, and these innovations pave the way for a brighter and more interconnected future.

The realm of information and education has undergone a revolutionary transformation, transcending the boundaries of traditional learning methods. This chapter invites you to embark on a journey into the dynamic and expansive world of e-books, online courses, and applications, collectively shaping the future of knowledge acquisition and personal development.

The internet and digital technologies have ushered in a renaissance in accessing, consuming, and disseminating information. Once a futuristic concept, E-books have become integral components of our digital libraries, providing unparalleled convenience and accessibility. In this chapter, we explore the evolution of e-books, delving into their impact on reading habits, publishing, and the democratization of knowledge.

Traditional classrooms are no longer the exclusive arenas for learning. Online courses have emerged as powerful educational tools, transcending geographical limitations and time constraints. As we navigate the expansive landscape of virtual classrooms, we will uncover online courses' benefits, challenges, and transformative potential, empowering learners to tailor their educational experiences to their unique needs and goals.

In an era dominated by smartphones and smart devices, applications have become indispensable companions on our digital journey. From language learning to fitness tracking, productivity enhancement, to mental well-being, apps have permeated every facet of our lives. This chapter examines the role of apps as catalysts for personal growth, providing insights into the diverse array of tools available to enhance our skills, knowledge, and overall quality of life.

E-books, online courses, and apps are not isolated entities; they converge at the intersection of technologies, creating synergies that redefine the learning experience. Augmented reality, artificial intelligence, and interactive multimedia are just a few technologies shaping the future of education and self-improvement. This chapter explores the innovative ways these technologies are harnessed to create immersive and engaging learning environments.

While the digital frontier presents boundless opportunities, it has challenges. Privacy concerns, information overload, and the digital divide are issues that demand thoughtful consideration. As we navigate this brave new world, we will also explore strategies for harnessing the vast potential while mitigating the risks, ensuring that the benefits of the digital age are accessible to all.

Embark with us on exploring the world of e-books, courses, and apps. This exploration transcends the boundaries of conventional education and embraces the limitless possibilities the digital revolution offers. Together, we will unravel the threads of innovation and discovery that weave the fabric of our ever-evolving quest for knowledge and personal growth.

The marriage of technology and literature has birthed a new era in how we consume, create, and interact with written content. This chapter will explore the dynamic intersection of technology and literature, focusing on the fascinating world of e-books, courses, and apps.

The advent of e-books has revolutionized the traditional reading experience. E-books, or electronic books, provide readers the convenience of carrying an entire library. The portability of e-readers, tablets, and smartphones has transformed how people engage with literature. Readers can access a vast array of titles with just a few taps, transcending geographical limitations and opening doors to a global literary landscape.

Moreover, the interactive nature of e-books has given rise to enhanced reading experiences. Hyperlinks, multimedia elements, and annotations empower readers to delve deeper into the narrative. Annotations can now be shared instantly, fostering a sense of community among readers who engage in virtual book clubs and discussions. This digital connectivity is reshaping the solitary act of reading into a collaborative and socially enriched endeavor.

The fusion of technology and education has paved the way for many online courses catering to literary enthusiasts and aspiring writers. The digital realm offers diverse learning and skill development opportunities, from creative writing workshops to literature appreciation courses.

Platforms like Coursera, Udemy, and Khan Academy have democratized access to literary education. Aspiring writers can refine their craft through virtual workshops conducted by acclaimed authors, while literature enthusiasts can deepen their understanding of literary theory and analysis. The convenience of asynchronous learning allows participants to engage with course content at their own pace, breaking down traditional barriers to education.

Mobile applications dedicated to literature are reshaping the way readers engage with content. Reading apps offer customizable interfaces, allowing users to personalize their reading experience. Features such as adjustable fonts, background colors, and interactive annotations cater to diverse reading preferences.

Apps like Goodreads have evolved into social platforms where readers can share book recommendations and reviews and connect with like-minded bibliophiles. Virtual bookshelves and personalized reading challenges add a gamified element to the reading experience, fostering a sense of accomplishment and community.

In addition to social platforms, apps like Audible have popularized audiobooks, allowing users to consume literature in a format that suits their busy lifestyles. This audio-centric approach has not only expanded the accessibility of literature but has also given rise to a new form of storytelling that blends narration, sound effects, and music.

While integrating technology with literature brings numerous advantages, it has challenges. Issues such as digital piracy, concerns about data privacy, and the potential loss of the tangible book experience continue to be debated.

However, these challenges are accompanied by a myriad of opportunities. Self-publishing platforms empower authors to share their stories without traditional gatekeepers. Virtual reality and augmented reality applications present possibilities for immersive storytelling experiences, bridging the gap between the digital and physical worlds.

The intersection of technology and literature has created a dynamic and ever-evolving landscape. E-books, courses, and apps have not replaced traditional forms of literary engagement but have expanded the horizons of what is possible. As we navigate this digital realm, embracing the opportunities that technology presents while preserving the essence of the written word that has captivated hearts and minds for centuries is essential. The fusion of technology and literature is a journey, and as we move forward, the possibilities for storytelling and literary exploration are boundless.

Turning Your Knowledge into Digital Assets

The digital landscape has revolutionized how we access and consume information and has provided unprecedented opportunities for individuals to transform their expertise into valuable digital assets. This chapter delves into the dynamic realm of turning knowledge into digital assets, exploring its profound impact on personal and professional growth.

We find ourselves in a knowledge economy, where information is the currency that fuels innovation, economic progress, and individual success. The traditional boundaries of education and expertise have expanded, and leveraging one's knowledge has become a key determinant of success in various fields.

The advent of the digital age has ushered in a renaissance of sorts, where the barriers to entry for disseminating information have crumbled. The internet, coupled with technological advancements, has democratized access to knowledge, allowing individuals to share their insights with a global audience instantaneously.

Digital assets, once confined to tangible entities like software and media files, now encompass a vast array of intellectual property, including courses, e-books, podcasts, and more. This chapter explores the evolution of digital assets, from simple text documents to immersive multimedia experiences, and the diverse formats in which knowledge can be packaged and delivered.

Turning your knowledge into digital assets isn't merely a technological feat; it's a strategic move that unlocks numerous opportunities. Whether you are an expert in a specific field, an entrepreneur, or an educator, the ability to package and distribute your knowledge digitally opens doors to new revenue streams, collaboration possibilities, and avenues for influence.

Embracing the concept of turning knowledge into digital assets requires adopting a digital entrepreneurial mindset. This mindset involves recognizing the value of your expertise, understanding the digital landscape, and strategically positioning your knowledge for maximum impact.

As with any transformative journey, challenges abound. From navigating intellectual property concerns to staying abreast of rapidly evolving technologies, this chapter addresses the potential hurdles and offers insights into overcoming them.

Beyond immediate gains, the creation of digital assets contributes to a lasting legacy. As you share your knowledge with the world, you influence the present and leave a mark on the future. This chapter explores the concept of crafting a digital legacy and the enduring impact it can have on generations to come.

Embark on this exploration of turning your knowledge into digital assets and discover the transformative potential within the convergence of knowledge, technology, and entrepreneurship. The following chapters will delve deeper into the strategies, tools, and principles that can guide you on this empowering journey.

In the modern era, the digital landscape offers an unprecedented opportunity for individuals to share their knowledge with a global audience. Creating online courses is one of the most effective ways to do this. This chapter will guide you through developing online courses and transforming your expertise into a valuable digital asset.

Before diving into course development, clearly define the expertise you want to share. Consider your unique skills, experiences, and knowledge that can provide genuine value to your audience.

Know your target audience. What are their needs, pain points, and aspirations? Tailoring your course to address specific challenges ensures its relevance and appeal.

Establishing clear learning objectives is crucial. What should your learners be able to do after completing the course? Objectives create a roadmap for you and your students, enhancing the learning experience.

Selecting a suitable platform is essential for the success of your online course. Popular platforms include Udemy, Teachable, and Coursera. Each has its features and audience, so choose one that aligns with your goals.

Organize your content logically. Start with an introduction, followed by modules or sections, and conclude with a summary or quiz. Ensure a natural flow that facilitates learning without overwhelming your students.
Use a variety of content types to keep your audience engaged. Combine video lectures, written content, quizzes, and interactive elements. Consider including real-life examples and case studies to make your content relatable and practical.

Leverage multimedia elements to enhance learning. High-quality visuals, infographics, and animations can significantly improve content comprehension and retention.

Engage your learners with interactive elements like quizzes, discussions, and assignments. Interaction fosters a sense of community and helps reinforce learning.

Ensure your course is accessible to a diverse audience. Use subtitles for videos, provide alternative text for images, and choose a platform that supports accessibility features.

Launch your course as a minimum viable product (MVP) and gather feedback. Continuously iterate based on learner input to enhance the quality and effectiveness of your content.

Develop a marketing strategy to promote your course effectively. Utilize social media, email campaigns, and partnerships to reach a wider audience. Consider offering introductory promotions to attract initial students.

Encourage community building around your course. Establish a discussion forum or social media group where learners can interact, share insights, and support each other.

Use analytics tools provided by your chosen platform to track student engagement, completion rates, and feedback. Analyzing data helps you understand what works and where improvements are needed.

Stay relevant by updating your course content regularly. Technology and knowledge evolve; your course should reflect these changes to maintain its value over time.

Understand the legal aspects of creating and selling online courses. Ensure you have the right to use any third-party content and protect your intellectual property.

Developing online courses is a dynamic process requiring expertise, technology, and continuous improvement. By carefully crafting your content, engaging with your audience, and adapting to changes, you can turn your knowledge into a valuable digital asset that benefits you and your learners. Embrace the journey of online course development, and watch as your expertise transforms into a widely accessible and impactful resource.

Congratulations! You've reached a pivotal moment in your journey to transform your expertise into a digital asset—launching your membership site. This chapter will guide you through the process, from planning and preparation to the launch. Buckle up, as this step will bring your vision to life and open the doors to a community eager to access and benefit from your knowledge.

Before launching, crystallize what your membership site will offer. Will it provide exclusive content, courses, webinars, or a combination? Clarify the value proposition for your audience. Identify the key benefits members will receive and how these offerings differ from elsewhere.

Selecting the right platform is crucial for the success of your membership site. Popular choices include platforms like MemberPress, Teachable, and Kajabi. Evaluate each platform based on ease of use, payment processing capabilities, and scalability. Ensure that the platform aligns with your goals and provides the necessary features to deliver a seamless experience to your members.

Create a sense of excitement by setting a launch date for your membership site. Building anticipation can be achieved through teaser content, sneak peeks, and behind-the-scenes glimpses. Utilize your existing channels, such as social media and email newsletters, to keep your audience engaged and informed about the upcoming launch.

Content is king, especially in the realm of membership sites. Develop high-quality content showcasing your expertise and offering your audience real value. Consider producing exclusive content for your members, such as in-depth tutorials, downloadable resources, or live Q&A sessions. This exclusive content will serve as a magnet, attracting individuals to become paying members.

Determine a fair and competitive pricing structure for your membership site. Consider factors such as the value you're providing, the level of exclusivity, and what your target audience is willing to pay. Additionally, decide on the monthly, quarterly, or annual payment frequency. Be transparent about your pricing to build trust with potential members.

A user-friendly website is essential for retaining members and encouraging new sign-ups. Ensure that the design is intuitive, navigation is seamless, and information is easily accessible. Optimize your website for desktop and mobile experiences to cater to a diverse audience.

Craft a comprehensive marketing strategy to promote your membership site. Leverage various channels like social media, email marketing, and partnerships. Consider offering limited-time promotions or early-bird discounts to incentivize early sign-ups. Use compelling language and visuals that highlight the benefits of becoming a member.

Excellent customer support is crucial for member retention. Establish clear communication channels for members to reach out with questions or concerns. Consider creating a community forum or group where members can connect, share insights, and support each other.

As the launch day arrives, celebrate your achievement. Send launch announcements, share success stories, and thank your founding members. Simultaneously, closely monitor the launch—track sign-ups, promptly address technical issues, and gather feedback to enhance the user experience.

After the launch, the journey is far from over. Continuously gather feedback from your members and iterate on your offerings. Consider introducing new content, refining existing features, and addressing pain points. The ability to adapt and improve will contribute to the long-term success of your membership site.

Launching a membership site is an exciting venture, transforming your knowledge into a valuable digital asset. These steps will create a platform for sharing your expertise and cultivating a community of engaged and dedicated members. Embrace the journey, learn from the experience, and enjoy the fulfillment of turning your knowledge into a sustainable and impactful digital venture.

In the ever-evolving landscape of digital assets, podcasting, and audio content have emerged as powerful tools for turning your knowledge into valuable digital assets. This chapter explores the world of podcasting, providing insights into how you can leverage this medium to share your expertise and create a lasting impact.

Podcasting has witnessed a meteoric rise in popularity over the past decade. Its accessibility, convenience, and the intimate connection it establishes with listeners make it a compelling platform for knowledge dissemination. Whether an expert in a specific field or a passionate enthusiast, podcasting allows you to reach a global audience quickly.

Identifying your niche is crucial when venturing into podcasting. Consider what you're passionate about and where your expertise lies. This could be anything from technology and science to self-improvement or business strategies. A focused niche helps you stand out and attract a dedicated audience.

A well-structured podcast requires careful planning. Outline your episodes, ensuring a logical flow of content. Consider incorporating interviews, case studies, and practical examples to engage your audience. Consistency is critical; establish a regular release schedule to build anticipation and loyalty.

While you don't need a professional studio, investing in decent recording equipment can significantly enhance the quality of your podcast. A good microphone, headphones, and soundproofing measures provide a more professional and enjoyable listening experience.

Your voice is your primary tool in podcasting. Work on your delivery, tone, and pacing to engage your audience. A conversational and authentic style often resonates well with listeners. Feel free to inject humor or personal anecdotes to make your content relatable.

Turning your podcast into a digital asset goes beyond just sharing knowledge; it can also be lucrative.

As your podcast gains traction, consider partnering with sponsors relevant to your niche. Sponsored content and advertisements can generate revenue, allowing you to monetize your expertise.

Create a sense of exclusivity by offering premium content or memberships. This could include bonus episodes, behind-the-scenes insights, or access to a community of like-minded individuals. Platforms like Patreon make it easy to set up subscription models.

Transform your audio content into written form through transcriptions. This not only enhances accessibility but also opens avenues for repurposing your knowledge into articles, e-books, or online courses.

Foster a sense of community by actively engaging with your audience. Encourage listener feedback, answer questions, and consider featuring audience contributions in your episodes. This not only strengthens your connection with listeners but also provides valuable content.

As technology advances, the podcasting landscape continues to evolve. Stay abreast of emerging trends like interactive podcasts, virtual reality experiences, and artificial intelligence integration. Embrace innovation to keep your podcast at the forefront of the digital content ecosystem.

Podcasting presents a dynamic and accessible avenue for turning your knowledge into a valuable digital asset. By carefully crafting your content, optimizing delivery, and exploring monetization strategies, you can share your expertise and build a sustainable and impactful presence in the digital realm.

Turning your knowledge into a valuable digital asset involves more than just creating written content. Webinars and workshops provide dynamic platforms for sharing expertise, engaging with your audience, and converting your knowledge into a valuable digital product. This chapter will guide you through conceptualizing, planning, and executing webinars and workshops to transform your expertise into a digital asset.

Before diving into the logistics, defining the purpose of your webinar or workshop is crucial. Are you aiming to educate, inspire, or provide practical skills? Understanding your objectives will shape the content and structure of your event. Consider the specific knowledge you want to share and the key takeaways for your audience.

Knowing your audience is essential for crafting content that resonates. Define your target demographic, understand their needs, and tailor your webinar or workshop to address their challenges. This will enhance engagement and increase the likelihood of your audience valuing your digital asset.

Your content is the heart of your webinar or workshop. Create a compelling narrative that takes your audience from understanding a concept to applying it. Incorporate multimedia elements such as slides, videos, and interactive activities to keep participants engaged. Balance theoretical concepts with practical examples to provide a comprehensive learning experience.

Selecting the right platform is crucial for the success of your digital event. Consider factors like ease of use, audience reach, and interactive features. Popular platforms like Zoom, Microsoft Teams, and WebEx offer various functionalities for hosting webinars and workshops. Choose one that aligns with your objectives and provides a seamless experience for you and your audience.

A well-executed plan and effective promotion are crucial to attracting participants. Develop a detailed timeline that includes content creation, technical checks, and rehearsal time. Leverage various promotional channels, such as social media, email newsletters, and your website, to create awareness and generate interest. Offering early-bird discounts or exclusive bonuses can incentivize registration.

Interactivity is vital for keeping your audience engaged throughout the event. Incorporate polls, Q&A sessions, and interactive discussions to foster participation. Encourage attendees to share their insights and experiences, creating a sense of community. Consider incorporating breakout sessions or group activities to enhance collaboration and networking.

Recording your webinar or workshop lets you repurpose the content into other digital assets. Create a polished version for on-demand access or transform segments into bite-sized videos for social media. This extends the lifespan of your knowledge, reaching a broader audience over time.

The relationship with your audience continues even after the webinar or workshop concludes. Foster ongoing engagement by providing additional resources, exclusive content, or a community platform for discussion. Gather feedback to improve future events and understand your audience's evolving needs.

If you want to generate revenue from your knowledge, explore monetization options. Offer paid access to premium content, provide certificates of completion, or bundle webinars and workshops into comprehensive courses. Implementing a monetization strategy adds value to your digital asset and helps you capitalize on your expertise.

Finally, treat each webinar or workshop as a learning experience. Analyze participant feedback, assess engagement metrics, and identify areas for improvement. This iterative process ensures that each digital asset you create becomes more valuable and impactful over time.

Webinars and workshops are powerful tools for transforming knowledge into digital assets. Understanding your audience, crafting compelling content, and leveraging the right platforms can create engaging and valuable experiences that educate and contribute to your digital success.

Chapter 7: The Power of Dividends

The power of dividends is often underestimated and overshadowed by the allure of capital gains. Investors, especially those with a long-term perspective, understand that dividends play a crucial role in building wealth, providing a steady income stream, and contributing to the overall stability of a portfolio.

Dividends represent a portion of a company's profits distributed to its shareholders. Unlike capital gains, which depend on the stock's price appreciation, dividends offer a tangible and regular return on investment. Companies that consistently pay dividends are often viewed as financially stable and well-established, as they have the cash flow to reward their investors.

One of the primary benefits of dividends is the consistent income they provide. Investors, particularly retirees, appreciate the reliability of regular dividend payments. By investing in dividend-paying stocks or dividend-focused funds, individuals can create a reliable income stream that can supplement their other sources of income, such as pensions or social security.

The real power of dividends lies in their ability to contribute to compound growth. Instead of cashing out dividends, investors can reinvest them into the same stock or other investments. By doing so, investors benefit from the compounding effect, where dividends generate additional income, which, in turn, leads to more dividends.

For example, suppose you own shares of a company that pays an annual dividend of $1 per share. If you reinvest those dividends to purchase additional shares, you will receive dividends on your original investment and the new shares. Over time, this compounding effect can significantly boost the overall return on your investment.

Dividend-paying stocks often demonstrate more stability during market downturns compared to non-dividend-paying stocks. The income generated from dividends can act as a cushion, helping to offset losses in the stock's market value. This stability is precious during economic downturns or periods of market volatility, providing investors with a sense of security and reducing the overall risk of their portfolios.

Investors seeking to harness the power of dividends should focus on companies with a history of consistent dividend payments and a solid financial position. Additionally, paying attention to metrics such as dividend yield, payout ratio, and the company's dividend growth rate can help evaluate the sustainability and potential for future dividend increases.

The power of dividends is a force that should not be underestimated in investing. Beyond the immediate income they provide, dividends contribute to the long-term growth of an investment portfolio through the magic of compounding. Investors who recognize and leverage the power of dividends can build a resilient and income-generating portfolio that stands the test of time, providing financial security and peace of mind. As the saying goes, "Don't just count on the market; let the market count for you," and dividends play a pivotal role in making that happen.

Dividend Investing: An Evergreen Passive Income Strategy

Dividend investing has stood the test of time as a robust and evergreen strategy for generating passive income. This chapter explores the enduring appeal of dividend investing, its historical significance, and the fundamental principles that make it a reliable source of wealth accumulation.

Dividend investing traces its roots back to the earliest days of stock markets. Companies have been distributing profits to their shareholders through dividends for centuries. The allure of regular cash payments, regardless of market conditions, has attracted investors through various economic cycles.

During the Industrial Revolution, when the modern stock market began to take shape, dividends played a pivotal role in attracting capital for expansion and growth. Investors were drawn to companies with a history of consistent dividend payments, recognizing the stability and reliability of such income streams.

One of the primary reasons dividend investing has maintained its appeal is its ability to provide stability in the face of market volatility. While stock prices may fluctuate, companies committed to paying dividends demonstrate a financial strength that withstands economic downturns. This stability is precious for investors seeking a reliable income source, regardless of broader market conditions.

Dividend investing aligns with the principle of compounding, a powerful force in wealth creation. Reinvesting dividends allows investors to purchase additional shares, leading to an exponential growth in income over time. This compounding effect becomes more pronounced with a long-term perspective, emphasizing the importance of patience in dividend investing.

Dividend payments have historically outpaced inflation rates, making them an effective hedge against rising living costs. Companies that consistently increase their dividends provide investors with an income stream that has the potential to grow faster than the eroding effects of inflation, preserving the purchasing power of their wealth.

Investors often look for companies with a track record of consistently increasing dividends. These companies, known as "Dividend Aristocrats," have demonstrated their ability to navigate economic challenges and reward shareholders with regular dividend hikes. Investing in Dividend Aristocrats can be a cornerstone of a successful dividend strategy.

The dividend yield, calculated as the annual dividend per share divided by the stock price, is a crucial metric for dividend investors. While a high yield may seem attractive, it is essential to consider the sustainability of the dividend and the company's overall financial health.

Diversification is a fundamental principle in investing, and it holds for dividend portfolios. Spreading investments across different sectors and industries helps mitigate risk and ensures that strengths in others balance the impact of poor performance in one area.

As we look to the future, the appeal of dividend investing remains robust. The strategy has adapted to evolving market conditions and provides a reliable income stream for investors seeking long-term financial security. The principles of stability, compounding growth, and inflation protection position dividend investing as an evergreen passive income strategy for future generations.

Building a Dividend Portfolio for Long-Term Wealth

Pursuing long-term wealth creation is a fundamental goal for many individuals. As economic conditions evolve and financial markets undergo fluctuations, investors seek strategies that provide stability, consistent growth, and a reliable income stream. Building a dividend portfolio is a time-tested and prudent method for attaining enduring financial success among the myriad investment approaches available.

This chapter embarks on a comprehensive exploration of the principles, strategies, and benefits associated with constructing a dividend portfolio geared toward long-term wealth accumulation. Dividend investing, once regarded as a strategy favored by income-focused investors, has evolved into a cornerstone of wealth-building portfolios, attracting a diverse range of market participants, from seasoned investors to newcomers in the financial arena.

At the heart of dividend investing lies the concept of regular income generation through the distribution of profits by companies to their shareholders. Dividends represent a tangible return on investment, offering investors a steady cash flow that can be reinvested or used to meet financial needs. This chapter delves into the mechanics of dividends, exploring how they function as a reliable source of income and examining the historical significance of dividends in long-term wealth creation.

Crafting a successful dividend portfolio requires a discerning eye for selecting stocks with a track record of consistent dividend payments and a strong potential for future growth. Investors navigate various metrics, such as dividend yield, payout ratio, and dividend growth history, to identify companies aligning with their financial objectives. This section outlines the criteria for selecting dividend-paying stocks and provides insights into conducting thorough research to make informed investment decisions.

Diversification is a fundamental risk management strategy, and the construction of a dividend portfolio is no exception. This chapter emphasizes diversifying across sectors, industries, and geographic regions to mitigate risk and enhance the portfolio's resilience to market volatility. Real-world examples and case studies illustrate the benefits of a well-balanced and diversified dividend portfolio.

The powerful concept of compounding is central to the long-term success of a dividend portfolio. By reinvesting dividends, investors harness the ability of their money to generate additional earnings, leading to exponential growth over time. This section elucidates the mechanics of dividend reinvestment, showcasing how it accelerates wealth accumulation and magnifies the impact of compounding.

Investors must navigate economic cycles and market fluctuations in an ever-changing economic landscape. This chapter explores strategies for building a resilient dividend portfolio capable of weathering economic downturns and capitalizing on opportunities presented by market volatility.

As we embark on this exploration of building a dividend portfolio for long-term wealth, it is essential to recognize that this journey requires a blend of strategic planning, disciplined execution, and a commitment to sound investing principles. Through the following pages, we will delve deeper into each facet of dividend investing, equipping you with the knowledge and insights needed to construct a robust portfolio that stands the test of time.

Dividend investing is an evergreen and reliable approach for generating passive income. This chapter will delve into the fundamentals of dividend investing, exploring the reasons behind its enduring popularity and the tangible benefits it offers to investors.

Dividend investing involves building a portfolio of stocks from companies that distribute a portion of their earnings to shareholders in the form of dividends. Dividends are cash payments made regularly, often quarterly, and are a tangible way for companies to share their profits with investors. Investors can benefit from dividend income as a steady stream of passive cash flow.

When investors buy shares of a dividend-paying company, they become eligible to receive a portion of its profits. Companies with a history of consistent earnings may declare dividends, which are then distributed to shareholders based on the number of shares they own. Dividend payments can provide a reliable income stream, making them attractive to income-focused investors.

One crucial metric for dividend investors is the dividend yield, which represents the annual dividend income as a percentage of the stock's current price. A higher dividend yield generally indicates a more attractive income opportunity, but investors must also consider the sustainability and growth potential of the dividends.

Dividend investing offers a range of advantages, making it a compelling strategy for investors seeking both income and long-term growth.

One of the primary benefits of dividend investing is the consistent income stream it provides. Unlike relying solely on stock price appreciation for returns, dividends offer a reliable source of cash flow, which can be especially valuable in economic downturns or volatile market conditions.

Dividend payments often have the potential to outpace inflation, helping investors preserve their purchasing power over time. Companies that regularly increase their dividends can provide investors with a hedge against the eroding effects of inflation.

While dividend investing is renowned for its income-generating capabilities, it also presents an avenue for long-term capital appreciation. Companies prioritizing dividend payments are often financially stable and well-established, with the potential for sustained growth in dividends and stock value.

Reinvesting dividends through a dividend reinvestment plan (DRIP) allows investors to harness the power of compounding. By automatically reinvesting dividends to purchase additional shares, investors can accelerate the growth of their investment over time.

Despite its advantages, dividend investing is not without risks. Investors must be aware of potential pitfalls, such as the impact of economic downturns on companies' ability to maintain dividend payments and the risk of investing in high-yield stocks that may be unsustainable.

Dividend-paying stocks can be sensitive to economic conditions. Companies may face challenges maintaining dividend payments during economic downturns if their earnings decline. Investors should carefully assess the financial health of companies in their dividend portfolio.

Changes in interest rates can impact the attractiveness of dividend stocks. When interest rates rise, fixed-income investments may become more appealing relative to dividend-paying stocks, potentially leading to selling pressure on dividend stocks.

Constructing a diversified dividend portfolio involves carefully selecting dividend-paying stocks across various sectors. Investors may also consider factors such as dividend growth, payout ratio, and the company's overall financial health.

Diversifying across sectors helps reduce the impact of poor performance in a particular industry. A well-balanced dividend portfolio might include utilities, consumer goods, healthcare, and technology stocks.

Investors often look for "Dividend Aristocrats," companies with a consistent track record of increasing dividends for a specified number of years. These companies are often considered more stable and reliable in their dividend payments.

As an evergreen passive income strategy, dividend investing provides investors a unique combination of stability, income, and growth potential. By understanding the fundamentals and carefully navigating the risks, investors can harness the power of dividends to build a resilient and rewarding investment portfolio. As with any investment strategy, due diligence, ongoing research, and a long-term perspective are crucial to success in dividend investing.

Dividend investing is a time-tested strategy for building a steady and reliable passive income stream. Investors need to employ a thoughtful and disciplined approach when selecting dividend stocks. This chapter will explore the critical criteria and analysis methods for identifying promising dividend-paying stocks.

Before delving into the selection criteria, it's crucial to grasp the basics of dividends. Dividends are periodic payments a company makes to its shareholders as a portion of its profits. These payouts can serve as a reliable income stream for investors. However, not all companies pay dividends, and the sustainability and growth of these payments are pivotal considerations.

The dividend yield is the most straightforward metric for evaluating the income potential of a dividend stock. It is calculated by dividing the annual dividend per share by the stock's current market price. While a higher yield can be enticing, it's essential to consider it in the context of the company's overall health and prospects.

Examining a company's dividend history provides valuable insights into its commitment to returning value to shareholders. Consistent and preferably growing dividends over the years indicate financial stability and management confidence. Look for companies with a history of maintaining or increasing dividends even during economic downturns.

The payout ratio is the proportion of a company's earnings paid out as dividends. A sustainable dividend stock typically has a moderate payout ratio, allowing the company to reinvest in its business and weather economic challenges. A lower payout ratio signifies room for future dividend increases.

Companies with a history of steady earnings growth are more likely to maintain and increase their dividend payments over time. Analyzing a company's financial reports and earnings forecasts helps assess its growth potential and the likelihood of sustaining dividend payments.

Solid fundamentals, including a healthy balance sheet, manageable debt levels, and positive cash flow, are crucial for the long-term viability of dividend payments. A company with a solid financial foundation can navigate market fluctuations and economic uncertainties better.

Beyond numerical metrics, qualitative factors play a vital role in selecting dividend stocks.

Consider the industry in which the company operates. Specific sectors are more stable and conducive to consistent dividend payments. Industries with long-term growth prospects may offer better opportunities for sustained dividend income.

Evaluate the company's competitive position within its industry. A market leader with a durable competitive advantage will likely generate stable profits and maintain dividends.

Assess the competence and track record of the company's management. A capable leadership team is essential for navigating challenges and making strategic decisions contributing to sustained dividend growth.

Diversification is a crucial principle of prudent investing. Building a diversified portfolio of dividend stocks across various sectors helps mitigate risks associated with industry-specific downturns and economic cycles.

Investors should regularly review their dividend portfolios and stay informed about changes in the companies they hold. Economic conditions, shifts in industry trends, and alterations in a company's financial health can all impact the sustainability of dividends.

Selecting dividend stocks involves a comprehensive analysis of both quantitative and qualitative factors. Investors can build a well-rounded portfolio that provides a reliable and growing stream of passive income by considering dividend yield, history, payout ratio, earnings growth, and fundamental strength. Additionally, ongoing monitoring and adjustment ensure the portfolio remains aligned with the investor's financial goals and market conditions. In the ever-evolving landscape of investing, dividend stocks stand out as an evergreen strategy for those seeking a consistent and enduring source of passive income.

Diversification is a fundamental principle in investing that aims to manage risk by spreading investments across different assets. In dividend investing, diversification is crucial in building a resilient and sustainable portfolio. As investors seek to create an evergreen passive income stream through dividends, employing effective diversification strategies becomes paramount.

Diversification is not merely about owning many stocks but constructing a well-balanced portfolio across various sectors, industries, and asset classes. In the context of dividend investing, diversification serves multiple purposes:

Various economic factors influence different sectors and industries. Diversifying across these segments helps mitigate the impact of adverse events on the overall portfolio. For example, if one sector experiences a downturn, dividends from other sectors may help offset potential losses.

Dependence on a single stock or sector for dividends can be risky. Companies may reduce or suspend dividends due to industry-specific challenges. By diversifying, investors create a more stable income stream, as disruptions in one sector are balanced by income from others.

Diversification isn't just about immediate risk management; it also sets the stage for long-term growth. By investing in a range of sectors, investors position themselves to capitalize on opportunities for growth in different segments of the economy.

- Allocate investments across various sectors such as technology, healthcare, consumer goods, and utilities.

- Consider the economic cycles and diversify into cyclical and non-cyclical sectors to balance the impact of economic fluctuations.

- Invest in companies from different regions and countries to reduce exposure to regional economic risks.

- Consider currency risks when investing internationally and diversify currency exposure to manage these risks.

- Diversify across different market capitalizations, including large-cap, mid-cap, and small-cap stocks.

- Each category has its risk-return profile, and a mix can provide a more balanced portfolio.

- To complement dividend stocks, consider including other income-generating assets, such as real estate investment trusts (REITs) or dividend-paying bonds.

- Diversifying into multiple asset classes adds another layer of protection against market volatility.

- Focus on companies with a consistent track record of increasing dividends, known as Dividend Aristocrats or Achievers.

- These companies often demonstrate financial stability and will likely continue providing reliable dividends.

- Regularly assess and reassess the risk profile of the portfolio.

- Monitor the correlation between different holdings to ensure proper diversification, as some stocks may move in tandem during market stress.

Diversification is a dynamic process that requires ongoing attention and adjustment. As investors navigate the world of dividend investing, applying thoughtful diversification strategies enhances the potential for building a resilient and evergreen passive income stream. By embracing a diversified approach, investors can better weather market uncertainties and position themselves for long-term success in dividend investing.

Dividend investing is not just about receiving periodic payouts from your investments; it's also about harnessing the incredible power of compounding to grow your wealth exponentially. Reinvesting dividends is a fundamental strategy that can turn a modest income stream into a formidable financial force, creating a perpetual cycle of wealth accumulation. In this chapter, we'll explore the dynamics of reinvesting dividends and how it contributes to the evergreen passive income strategy of dividend investing.

Dividend reinvestment involves using the dividends received from your investments to purchase additional shares of the same stock or fund. Instead of taking the cash payout, you can plow those earnings back into the investment that generated them. This seemingly simple choice creates a compounding process that can profoundly impact your long-term returns.

Compounding is often called the "eighth wonder of the world" for a good reason. When you reinvest dividends, you're earning returns on your initial investment and the returns generated by your reinvested dividends. As your investment base grows, this creates a snowball effect, and each subsequent dividend payout contributes to an increasingly more significant sum.

Let's consider a hypothetical scenario to illustrate the compounding magic. Imagine you own a company that pays an annual dividend of $2 per share, and the stock has an average yearly return of 8%. If you reinvest your dividends, you receive additional shares and earn returns on those reinvested dividends. Over time, the compounding effect accelerates, turning a steady stream of dividends into a substantial wealth-building engine.

Reinvesting dividends can also act as a buffer against short-term market fluctuations. During market downturns, the reinvested dividends continue accumulating additional shares at potentially lower prices. This dollar-cost averaging approach helps smooth out the impact of market volatility, positioning investors to benefit when markets eventually recover.

The beauty of reinvesting dividends is its ability to create a self-reinforcing cycle. As your investment grows, so does the income generated by your portfolio. The increased income, in turn, allows you to acquire more shares, leading to even more incredible future income. This virtuous cycle can continue to compound over the years, creating a source of passive income that can be both resilient and sustainable.

There are various ways to implement dividend reinvestment strategies. Some investors automatically reinvest dividends through dividend reinvestment plans (DRIPs), which many companies offer. Others may prefer to manually reinvest dividends based on their investment goals and market conditions.

Reinvesting dividends is a powerful tool in the arsenal of dividend investors. By harnessing the force of compounding, investors can transform a steady income stream into a growing asset base. The compounding effect amplifies returns over time and provides a cushion against market volatility. As you embark on your dividend investing journey, consider the long-term benefits of reinvesting dividends and the potential for compounding to work in your favor. In investing, time and patience can be your greatest allies, and reinvesting dividends is a strategy that rewards both.

Congratulations on establishing your dividend portfolio! As you embark on your dividend-investing journey, you must recognize that your work doesn't end with the initial selection of dividend-paying stocks. Monitoring and adjusting your portfolio is crucial to maintaining a healthy and profitable investment strategy. This chapter will explore the critical elements of managing your dividend portfolio for long-term success.

Dividend investing is not a set-it-and-forget-it strategy. The financial markets are dynamic and influenced by economic conditions, industry trends, and company-specific factors. Regularly monitoring your dividend portfolio ensures you stay informed about changes that may impact your investments.

Set a routine for reviewing your portfolio. This could be quarterly, semi-annually, or annually, depending on your preference and the time you can commit. During these reviews, evaluate the performance of each stock, considering factors such as dividend yield, payout ratio, and overall financial health of the companies in your portfolio.

Check if the companies in your portfolio are maintaining or, ideally, increasing their dividends over time. A consistent dividend payment history is a positive sign, indicating a company's financial strength and stability. Be wary of companies with fluctuating or decreasing dividends, as this may be a red flag.

Stay informed about economic trends and changes in the industries of the companies you've invested in. Economic downturns or shifts in industry dynamics can impact a company's ability to sustain its dividend payments. Adjust your portfolio accordingly by diversifying across sectors or reallocating funds based on the economic outlook.

Over time, the market value of individual stocks in your portfolio may change, leading to an imbalance in your original asset allocation. Rebalancing involves buying or selling assets to restore your portfolio to its intended allocation. This process helps manage risk and ensures that your portfolio aligns with your investment goals.

Be open to adjusting your investment strategy based on changing market conditions or personal financial goals. If a stock no longer meets your criteria for dividend investing, consider selling it and reallocating the funds to a more promising opportunity.

Understand the tax implications of your dividend investments. Different jurisdictions have varying tax treatment for dividends. Consider consulting with a tax professional to optimize your portfolio for tax efficiency.

The stock market can be unpredictable, and emotions like fear and greed can cloud judgment. Stay disciplined and make decisions based on thorough analysis and your long-term investment objectives. Avoid making impulsive decisions in response to short-term market fluctuations.

Monitoring and adjusting your dividend portfolio is a continuous process that requires diligence and strategic thinking. By staying informed, regularly reviewing your investments, and being adaptable, you can maximize the potential for long-term success with your dividend portfolio. When managed effectively, dividend investing is an evergreen passive income strategy that can provide financial stability and growth.

Chapter 8: The Art of Affiliate Marketing

Affiliate marketing is an art form that blends creativity, strategy, and technology to create a harmonious symphony of revenue generation. In this chapter, we'll delve into the intricacies of the affiliate marketing landscape, exploring the fundamental principles, best practices, and innovative strategies that can elevate your affiliate marketing game to new heights.

Affiliate marketing operates within a vast ecosystem that involves merchants, affiliates, and consumers. Merchants offer products or services, affiliates promote them, and consumers purchase through affiliate links. To excel in this art, one must comprehend the roles of each player and how they interconnect.

Merchants are the creators or providers of products/services. They set up affiliate programs to expand their reach and boost sales. A successful affiliate marketer must choose reputable merchants whose products align with their audience's interests.

Affiliates act as intermediaries between merchants and consumers. They promote products through various channels, earning a commission for every sale or lead generated. Diversifying the affiliate portfolio and selecting quality products are crucial for sustained success.

Understanding consumer behavior is pivotal. Affiliates must build trust with their audience, recommending products that genuinely add value. Authenticity and transparency are the building blocks of a lasting affiliate-consumer relationship.

At the heart of affiliate marketing lies content creation. Whether blog posts, videos, or social media updates, your content must resonate with your audience and seamlessly integrate affiliate links.

Craft compelling narratives around the products you promote. Share personal experiences, testimonials, or case studies to create a connection with your audience. People resonate with stories; a well-told tale can significantly boost conversion rates.

Authenticity is the linchpin of successful affiliate marketing. Only promote products you genuinely believe in. Your audience can sense insincerity, and trust is easily eroded. Be transparent about your affiliations, and your recommendations will carry more weight.

Successful affiliate marketers don't just scatter links randomly; they strategically position and promote them to maximize impact.

Identify and focus on a specific niche. Tailor your content and promotions to cater to your target audience's unique needs and interests. A niche approach often yields higher conversion rates.

Align your promotions with seasonal trends, holidays, or special events. This keeps your content fresh and relevant and capitalizes on heightened consumer interest during specific periods.

In the digital age, technology is a powerful ally. Harnessing the right tools and analytics can provide invaluable insights into your audience, the performance of your campaigns, and areas for improvement.

Invest in reliable affiliate tracking software to accurately monitor clicks, conversions, and commissions. This helps you optimize your strategy based on real-time data.

Experiment with different approaches to identify what resonates best with your audience. A/B testing your content, headlines, and calls to action can provide valuable insights into consumer preferences.

Affiliate marketing is not a one-time transaction; it's about building long-term relationships with your audience and merchant partners.

Communicate regularly with your affiliate managers. Understand the product roadmap, upcoming promotions, and any changes to commission structures. A strong relationship can open doors to exclusive deals and insights.

Foster a sense of community among your audience. Respond to comments, emails, and messages. Engage in conversations and seek feedback. The more connected your audience feels, the more likely they trust your recommendations.

The affiliate marketing landscape is dynamic, with trends and technologies evolving rapidly. To master this art, one must stay abreast of industry developments and be willing to adapt.

Explore new platforms and channels where your audience spends time. Whether it's TikTok, podcasts, or emerging social media, diversifying your presence can expand your reach.

Video content continues to dominate the online space. Incorporate video into your affiliate strategy, whether through product reviews, tutorials, or engaging storytelling.

Maintaining ethical standards is paramount in affiliate marketing. Disclose your affiliations transparently, adhere to regulations, and ensure that your promotions are truthful and compliant.

Understand and comply with the Federal Trade Commission (FTC) guidelines regarding affiliate marketing disclosures. Clearly state when you are using affiliate links, and avoid deceptive practices.

Thoroughly understand the products you promote. Misleading or inaccurate information damages your credibility and erodes trust with your audience.

The art of affiliate marketing is a dynamic and multifaceted discipline. It requires creativity, strategic thinking, and building genuine connections. By understanding the intricacies of the affiliate ecosystem, crafting compelling content, employing strategic promotions, leveraging technology, building relationships, staying adaptive, and maintaining ethical standards, you can truly master this art and create a sustainable and rewarding affiliate marketing journey. Remember, like any art form, mastery is a continuous process of learning, experimenting, and refining your approach.

Leveraging Partnerships for Passive Profits

In the ever-evolving landscape of business, the concept of collaboration and partnership has become increasingly vital. Entrepreneurs and business leaders realize that successful ventures often require a network of strategic alliances to thrive. Leveraging partnerships enhances the overall value proposition and opens avenues for passive profits. In this chapter, we'll explore the art of forging partnerships and how you can turn them into a source of passive income.

Partnerships are not just about expanding your reach; they're about creating synergies that benefit all parties involved. Before seeking partnerships, identify businesses or individuals whose strengths complement yours. This synergy is the foundation for long-term success and passive profits.

Selecting the right partners is a crucial step in creating a profitable collaboration. Consider partners who share your values, have a similar target audience, and bring unique strengths. Whether it's a joint venture, affiliate marketing, or co-branding initiative, aligning with the right partners is the key to a successful and sustainable partnership.

The agreements must be mutually beneficial to turn partnerships into a source of passive income. Clearly outline the roles, responsibilities, and expectations of each party involved. Establish transparent revenue-sharing models that incentivize both sides to contribute actively to the partnership's success.

One of the most effective ways to generate passive profits through partnerships is by incorporating affiliate marketing and referral programs. You create a win-win situation by allowing partners to promote your products or services and earn a commission on each sale or lead. This automated system will enable you to benefit from your partners' efforts without direct involvement.

Collaborative ventures, where partners jointly create and promote products or services, can generate substantial passive profits. This could involve co-hosting events, creating co-branded products, or developing joint marketing campaigns. The shared effort reduces individual costs and broadens the reach, increasing passive income potential.

To maximize passive profits, leverage technology to automate processes. Implement tracking systems, analytics, and automated payment solutions to streamline the partnership's performance monitoring and revenue distribution. This minimizes manual intervention, allowing you to focus on growing the partnership and exploring new collaborative opportunities.

Successful partnerships require ongoing communication and adaptation. Regularly assess the performance of your collaborations and make adjustments as needed. Stay informed about industry trends, market changes, and shifts in consumer behavior to ensure that your partnerships remain relevant and continue to generate passive income over time.

Avoid relying solely on one or two partnerships for passive profits. Diversify your collaboration portfolio to spread the risk and enhance your revenue streams. This approach safeguards your business against unforeseen challenges and opens up opportunities for exponential growth through multiple channels.

Ensure that all partnerships adhere to legal and ethical standards. Clearly define contract terms, address confidentiality issues, and establish dispute resolution mechanisms. A solid legal foundation protects your business interests and fosters trust between partners, contributing to the longevity of the collaboration.

Leveraging partnerships for passive profits is an ongoing journey that requires dedication, strategic thinking, and adaptability. As you build and nurture collaborative relationships, you'll discover new ways to generate passive income and unlock the full potential of your business ecosystem. Embrace the power of partnerships, and watch as your network becomes a sustainable source of passive profits for years.

Strategies for Successful Affiliate Marketing

Affiliate marketing has become integral to the digital landscape, allowing businesses and individuals to generate revenue through partnerships. As the competition in the online space continues to grow, it becomes crucial for affiliate marketers to adopt effective strategies to stand out and achieve success. This chapter will explore key strategies for a thriving affiliate marketing campaign.

Successful affiliate marketing begins with selecting the right niche. Focus on areas where you have expertise or a genuine interest. Understanding your target audience is vital; align your chosen niche with their needs and preferences. A well-defined niche helps you tailor your content and promotions effectively.

Content is the cornerstone of any successful affiliate marketing strategy. Create high-quality, valuable content that educates and engages your audience. Whether through blog posts, videos, or social media, establish yourself as an authority in your niche. This builds trust with your audience, making them more likely to follow your recommendations.

Before promoting any product or service, thoroughly understand it. Use the product or conduct in-depth research to provide accurate and honest reviews. Your credibility is at stake, and promoting products you believe in enhances your reputation as a trustworthy affiliate.

Relying on a single promotional channel is risky. Diversify your efforts across various platforms such as social media, email marketing, SEO, and paid advertising. This approach ensures a broader reach and protects your business from sudden changes in algorithms or policies on any particular platform.

Search engine optimization is crucial for long-term success. Optimize your content for relevant keywords and ensure your website is well-structured and user-friendly. Higher visibility on search engines not only attracts more organic traffic but also establishes your credibility in the eyes of your audience.

Social media platforms are powerful tools for affiliate marketers. Build a strong presence on platforms relevant to your niche, engage with your audience, and share valuable content. Leverage the reach of social media to drive traffic to your affiliate products.

Build an email list and use it wisely. Email marketing allows you to nurture relationships with your audience, share valuable content, and promote relevant affiliate products. Develop a strategy that includes a mix of informational and promotional emails to keep your subscribers engaged.

The digital landscape is dynamic, with trends and technologies evolving rapidly. Stay informed about changes in your niche and the affiliate marketing industry. Adapting to emerging trends keeps your strategies relevant and positions you as a forward-thinking marketer.

Regularly track the performance of your affiliate campaigns. Use analytics tools to assess which strategies are yielding the best results. Analyzing data allows you to optimize your approach, focusing on what works and refining or abandoning less effective methods.

Adhere to legal and ethical standards in affiliate marketing. Disclose your affiliate relationships to your audience, as transparency fosters trust. Comply with relevant regulations and guidelines to avoid legal issues and maintain a positive reputation.

Successful affiliate marketing requires a strategic and multifaceted approach. You can build a sustainable and profitable affiliate marketing business by choosing the right niche, creating valuable content, diversifying promotional channels, and staying informed about industry trends. Remember, consistency and adaptability are critical in this ever-evolving digital landscape.

Chapter 9: Automated Businesses and Dropshipping

Technological advancements are reshaping traditional business models. One of the most notable trends in recent years has been the rise of automated businesses, with dropshipping emerging as a critical player in this transformative wave.

Automation has become a cornerstone of efficiency in the business world. From manufacturing to customer service, businesses are leveraging technology to streamline processes and reduce human intervention. The automation revolution has reached its zenith with the birth of fully automated companies, where machines handle processes, transactions, and even decision-making.

Automated businesses significantly cut labor costs, allowing entrepreneurs to allocate resources elsewhere.

Machines operate with precision, minimizing errors and enhancing the overall quality of products or services.

Unlike human employees, automated systems don't need breaks or sleep. This enables businesses to operate around the clock, reaching global audiences in different time zones.

Dropshipping has become synonymous with the new age of commerce. In this business model, entrepreneurs act as intermediaries, selling products to customers without handling the physical inventory. Instead, products are shipped directly from suppliers to customers.

Entrepreneurs can start a dropshipping business with minimal upfront costs since they don't need to invest in inventory.

The dropshipping model allows for flexibility in product offerings, and businesses can quickly scale by adding or removing products from their online store.

With drop shipping, entrepreneurs can source products from suppliers worldwide, reaching a global customer base without needing a physical presence in different locations.

The fusion of automation and dropshipping has given birth to platforms that offer end-to-end solutions for aspiring entrepreneurs. These platforms handle everything from order processing and inventory management to customer support and marketing.

Artificial intelligence (AI) plays a pivotal role in the evolution of dropshipping. AI algorithms analyze consumer behavior, optimize pricing strategies, and personalize marketing campaigns. This data-driven approach enhances the customer experience and increases the likelihood of successful transactions.

Automated businesses, especially in the realm of dropshipping, face challenges related to quality control. Ensuring that products meet customer expectations can be a hurdle, and maintaining high customer satisfaction is crucial for long-term success.

As the popularity of automated businesses and dropshipping grows, markets can become saturated with similar products. Entrepreneurs must focus on differentiation, branding, and providing unique value to stand out in a crowded landscape.

The marriage of automation and dropshipping has ushered in a new era of entrepreneurship. As technology advances, the business landscape will undoubtedly evolve further. Entrepreneurs navigating this space must balance the benefits of automation with the challenges inherent in maintaining quality, customer satisfaction, and market differentiation. The future belongs to those who can harness the power of technology while staying attuned to consumers' ever-changing needs and expectations.

Exploring E-commerce Opportunities

In the rapidly evolving business landscape, e-commerce has emerged as a transformative force, reshaping how companies operate, and consumers engage with products and services. This chapter delves into the multifaceted world of e-commerce, examining the vast opportunities it presents for entrepreneurs, businesses, and consumers alike.

E-commerce, short for electronic commerce, refers to the buying and selling goods and services over the Internet. This dynamic platform has transcended geographical boundaries, enabling businesses to reach global markets efficiently. As technology advances, the opportunities within e-commerce continue to expand, providing fertile ground for innovation and growth.

Explore various e-commerce models, including Business-to-Consumer (B2C), Business-to-Business (B2B), Consumer-to-Consumer (C2C), and more. Each model comes with its unique set of opportunities, catering to different market needs and consumer behaviors.

With the ubiquity of smartphones, M-commerce has gained significant traction. Dive into the opportunities of mobile apps, mobile-optimized websites, and mobile payment solutions. Connecting with consumers on the go opens up new dimensions for businesses.

Online marketplaces like Amazon, eBay, and Alibaba provide a ready-made platform for sellers to reach a vast audience. Learn how businesses can leverage these marketplaces, the challenges they may encounter, and the strategies to stand out in a crowded marketplace.

For businesses looking to establish a distinct online presence, creating a dedicated e-commerce website is essential. Explore the opportunities and challenges of building and maintaining a custom website, including considerations like user experience, security, and payment gateways.

Effectively promoting products or services online requires a robust digital marketing strategy. Delve into SEO, social media marketing, email campaigns, and influencer partnerships. Understanding how to navigate these channels is critical to driving traffic and boosting sales.

E-commerce thrives on data. Learn how businesses can harness the power of analytics to understand consumer behavior, optimize marketing efforts, and enhance the overall customer experience. Real-time data insights enable businesses to adapt quickly to market trends.

One of the most compelling aspects of e-commerce is the potential for global reach. Explore the challenges and opportunities of expanding into international markets, including cultural considerations, logistics, and regulatory compliance.

Examine the role of emerging technologies like artificial intelligence, augmented reality, and blockchain in shaping the future of e-commerce. Understand how these technologies can enhance customer engagement, streamline operations, and provide a competitive edge.

No exploration of e-commerce opportunities is complete without addressing the challenges inherent in the digital landscape. From cybersecurity concerns to evolving consumer preferences, businesses must adapt to stay relevant. Additionally, discuss future trends such as voice commerce, virtual reality shopping experiences, and sustainability in e-commerce.

As e-commerce continues to evolve, so do the opportunities for businesses willing to embrace innovation and adapt to changing landscapes. By understanding the diverse facets of e-commerce, entrepreneurs and companies can position themselves to thrive in the dynamic world of online commerce. Whether venturing into new markets, adopting cutting-edge technologies, or refining marketing strategies, the possibilities within e-commerce are vast and exciting.

Setting Up a Successful Dropshipping Business

In the fast-paced world of e-commerce, dropshipping has emerged as a popular and low-risk business model for aspiring entrepreneurs. This chapter will guide you through the essential steps to set up a successful dropshipping business. From choosing the right niche to optimizing your website for conversions, each step plays a crucial role in determining your business's success.

- Begin by researching market trends and identifying products with high demand.

- Utilize tools like Google Trends, Amazon Best Sellers, and social media to gauge product popularity.

- Choose a niche that aligns with your interests and expertise. This will keep you motivated and engaged.

- Consider the potential for growth and the availability of reliable suppliers in your chosen niche.

- Analyze your competitors to understand their strengths and weaknesses.

- Identify gaps in the market that you can fill or areas where you can offer a unique value proposition.

- Define your target audience and create buyer personas.

- Understand the needs and preferences of your potential customers to tailor your marketing efforts.

- Seek reputable suppliers with a history of reliability and quality products.

- Communicate with potential suppliers to ensure they can meet your business requirements.

- Order samples from potential suppliers to evaluate product quality firsthand.

- Establish clear communication channels and agreements with your chosen suppliers.

- Select a user-friendly e-commerce platform such as Shopify, WooCommerce, or BigCommerce.

- Ensure the platform supports dropshipping and integrates seamlessly with your chosen suppliers.

- Create a visually appealing and easy-to-navigate website.

- Optimize product pages for conversions with high-quality images, compelling product descriptions, and clear calls to action.

- Leverage social media platforms to build brand awareness and engage your audience.

- Run targeted ads on platforms like Facebook and Instagram to drive traffic to your website.

- Develop a content strategy that includes blog posts, videos, and other valuable content related to your niche.

- Use SEO best practices to improve your website's visibility on search engines.

- Provide prompt and helpful customer service to build trust and loyalty.

- Set up clear communication channels and address customer inquiries and concerns promptly.

- Implement a reliable order tracking system to inform customers about their purchases.

- Work closely with your suppliers to ensure timely order fulfillment and delivery.

- Monitor key performance indicators (KPIs) such as conversion rates, traffic, and customer acquisition cost.

- Use analytics tools to gain insights into customer behavior and adjust your strategy accordingly.

- Explore expansion opportunities, such as adding new products or targeting additional markets.

- Consider automating certain aspects of your business to handle increased volume efficiently.

Setting up a successful dropshipping business requires careful planning, continuous learning, and adaptability. You can position your dropshipping business by selecting the right niche, building a reliable supplier network, optimizing your website, implementing effective marketing strategies, and providing excellent customer service. Stay informed about industry trends, embrace innovation, and be ready to adjust your strategy based on market dynamics. With dedication and a strategic approach, your dropshipping venture can thrive in the competitive e-commerce landscape.

Chapter 10: Mastering Passive Income through Passive Businesses

Mastering passive income through passive businesses has become an essential strategy for many entrepreneurs. Passive income offers the allure of generating money while you sleep, allowing you to pursue other passions, spend time with loved ones, or enjoy life. In this chapter, we will delve into the concept of passive businesses and explore practical strategies to create sustainable and reliable passive income streams.

Passive businesses are enterprises designed to generate income with minimal ongoing effort from the owner. These businesses typically require substantial upfront work, investment, or time commitment, but once established, they can operate with minimal day-to-day involvement. Common examples of passive businesses include rental properties, automated online businesses, dividend-paying investments, and affiliate marketing ventures.

Investing in real estate is a classic avenue for building passive income. You can earn regular income through monthly rent payments by acquiring rental properties. To maximize the passive nature of this business, consider hiring a property management company to handle day-to-day tasks like maintenance and tenant communication.

Additionally, real estate crowdfunding platforms allow investors to pool resources for larger projects, providing a more hands-off approach to property investment. The key is carefully researching and selecting properties with strong rental potential and growth prospects.

The digital age has given rise to numerous opportunities for passive income through online businesses. E-commerce stores, digital products, and affiliate marketing can be automated to a large extent. You can create systems that generate income without constant supervision by leveraging tools like marketing automation, chatbots, and e-commerce platforms.

Creating evergreen content, such as online courses or e-books, allows you to make money continuously as people discover and purchase your products. Outsourcing tasks like customer service and content creation can further streamline your online business operations.

Investing in dividend-paying stocks and funds is another way to build passive income. As companies generate profits, they may distribute a portion of those earnings to shareholders as dividends. You can create a reliable income stream by carefully selecting dividend-paying stocks and holding onto them long-term.

Diversification is crucial in this strategy to mitigate risks. Regularly reinvesting dividends can also accelerate wealth accumulation over time. Utilizing robo-advisors or working with a financial advisor can help you make informed investment decisions aligned with your financial goals.

Affiliate marketing involves promoting other people's products and earning a commission for each sale made through your referral. Building a successful affiliate marketing business requires creating valuable content, cultivating an audience, and strategically placing affiliate links.
To master passive income through affiliate marketing, focus on evergreen niches, create high-quality content that addresses your audience's needs, and optimize your website for search engines. Over time, as your content ranks and attracts organic traffic, your affiliate links can generate income without active promotion.

The key to mastering passive income is automation. Utilize technology and outsourcing to streamline your business operations. Delegate tasks that don't require direct involvement, allowing you to focus on strategic decisions and scaling your passive income streams.

The business landscape is dynamic, and what works today may be less effective tomorrow. Stay informed about industry trends, changes in consumer behavior, and emerging technologies. Continuous learning will enable you to adapt your passive business strategies for sustained success.

Choose passive income streams that can be scaled without proportional increases in time and effort. Whether it's expanding your real estate portfolio, growing your online business, or diversifying your investment portfolio, scalability is essential for maximizing the potential of passive income.

Building passive income through passive businesses requires patience. Results may take time, but with a long-term vision and commitment to your chosen strategies, you can achieve financial independence and enjoy the benefits of a truly passive income.

Mastering passive income through passive businesses is a journey that demands careful planning, strategic decision-making, and continuous adaptation. By understanding the principles behind passive income, leveraging suitable business models, and staying committed to your long-term goals, you can create a sustainable and reliable source of income that affords you the freedom to live on your terms. Remember, each individual's path to financial independence is unique, so tailor your approach to align with your values, preferences, and aspirations.

Creating Systems That Work for You

The importance of creating systems cannot be overstated. Systems are the backbone of productivity, providing structure and clarity to our daily routines. When tailored to our unique preferences and needs, these systems become powerful tools that empower us to navigate the complexities of our lives quickly.

Before delving into creating effective systems, it's crucial to understand why they are essential. Systems bring order to chaos, providing a framework for managing tasks, responsibilities, and goals. They help streamline processes, reduce decision fatigue, and enhance overall productivity. When thoughtfully designed, systems focus more on what truly matters, enabling individuals to channel their energy into meaningful and fulfilling pursuits.

The first step in creating systems that work for you is a thorough self-assessment. Understand your priorities, strengths, weaknesses, and the areas of your life that could benefit from increased organization. Consider your personal and professional goals and the values that guide your decision-making. This self-awareness will be the foundation for designing systems that align with your unique circumstances.
Start by breaking down your life into critical areas such as work, personal development, health, relationships, and leisure. This segmentation provides a clear overview of where your time and energy are allocated.

Define specific, measurable, and achievable goals for each area. Knowing what you want to accomplish provides a roadmap for creating systems that support your objectives.
Break down the processes involved in achieving your goals. Whether it's a daily workflow, project management, or a routine task, understanding the steps involved allows you to identify potential bottlenecks and areas for improvement.

Select tools and resources that complement your preferences and working style. Whether it's a task management app, a physical planner, or a combination of both, the right tools enhance the effectiveness of your systems.

Integrate routines into your systems to create consistency. Routines help automate certain aspects of your day, reducing the mental effort required for decision-making and increasing overall efficiency.

Regularly review your systems to assess their effectiveness. Be open to iteration and refinement as your needs and circumstances evolve.
Design workflows that prioritize tasks set deadlines, and incorporate breaks to maintain productivity. Utilize project management tools to track progress and collaborate with team members.

Establish routines for learning and skill development. Whether dedicating daily time to reading, attending workshops, or practicing a hobby, intentional systems foster continuous personal growth.

Create systems for meal planning, exercise routines, and regular health check-ups. Prioritize self-care by integrating practices that contribute to your physical and mental well-being.
Foster meaningful connections by scheduling regular time with loved ones. Implement communication strategies that align with your values, ensuring your relationships receive the attention they deserve.

Develop systems for downtime and relaxation. Whether scheduling regular breaks, planning vacations, or engaging in hobbies, intentional leisure systems contribute to a balanced and fulfilling life.

Creating systems is an ongoing process that requires adaptability and resilience. It's essential to stay open to change and be willing to modify your systems as needed. Additionally, be mindful of potential obstacles, such as procrastination, burnout, or unexpected life events, and adjust your systems accordingly.

The creation of tailored systems is a powerful tool. By understanding your unique needs, setting clear goals, and designing systems that align with your values, you empower yourself to navigate the complexities of life with intention and efficiency. As you implement and refine these systems, you'll be better equipped to achieve your goals, embrace new opportunities, and live a life that reflects your priorities. Remember, the journey to creating systems that work for you is a dynamic and evolving process, and the key is to remain committed to continuous improvement.

The Road to Business Automation

The journey toward efficiency and productivity is a perpetual quest. As technology advances at an unprecedented pace, organizations must explore innovative ways to streamline operations and stay competitive. The road to business automation is one of the most transformative avenues in this pursuit.

In its simplest form, automation involves using technology to perform tasks without human intervention. While the concept is not new, the scope and impact of automation have expanded significantly over the years. The early stages saw the mechanization of manual tasks in industries, laying the groundwork for more sophisticated processes in the digital age.

The advent of computers and software marked a pivotal moment, enabling businesses to automate repetitive and rule-based tasks.

However, the true catalyst for the automation revolution emerged with the rise of artificial intelligence (AI) and machine learning (ML). These technologies shifted paradigms, allowing systems to learn from data, adapt, and execute complex tasks with minimal human guidance.

The compelling reasons businesses embark on the road to automation are multifaceted. Chief among them is the pursuit of efficiency. Automation promises faster and more accurate execution of tasks, freeing up human resources to focus on strategic and creative endeavors.

Cost savings also loom large on the horizon. While the initial investment in automation technology might be significant, the long-term gains in reduced operational costs, error mitigation, and increased output often far outweigh the upfront expenses. Moreover, as technology advances, the cost of implementing automation solutions gradually decreases, making it more accessible to businesses of all sizes.

Automation is a crucial enabler of data-driven decision-making in a world where data reigns supreme. Automated systems can analyze vast datasets at speeds beyond human capacity, extracting actionable insights and fostering a more informed approach to business strategies.

While the benefits of automation are undeniable, the journey toward its implementation is not without its challenges. The first step on this road is a comprehensive assessment of existing processes. Identifying repetitive, time-consuming, and error-prone tasks lays the foundation for determining where automation can have the most significant impact.

Selecting the right technology is a critical decision. Businesses must evaluate their specific needs and objectives before choosing between robotic process automation (RPA), AI-driven solutions, or a combination. Integrating automation into existing systems requires careful planning to ensure a seamless transition and minimal disruption.

Employee buy-in is another pivotal factor. The successful implementation of automation hinges on a workforce that embraces and understands the technology. Clear communication, training programs, and ongoing support are essential to alleviate concerns and foster a culture that welcomes automation as a tool for empowerment rather than a threat to job security.

As businesses traverse the road to automation, the future landscape promises even more incredible advancements. Automation synergy with emerging technologies like the Internet of Things (IoT), blockchain, and 5G will open new possibilities. Intelligent, interconnected systems will redefine how businesses operate, creating an environment where real-time data, predictive analytics, and autonomous decision-making become the norm.

In conclusion, the road to business automation is not a destination but a continuous journey of adaptation and innovation. As technology continues to evolve, businesses that embrace automation as a strategic imperative will survive and thrive in the dynamic landscape of the future. The era of human-machine collaboration is upon us, and those who navigate this road wisely will pave the way for a new era of efficiency, agility, and sustained success.

Chapter 11: Making the Most of Royalties and Licensing

The concept of royalties and licensing has become increasingly vital. Artists, authors, musicians, inventors, and even businesses rely on the income generated through royalties and licensing agreements to protect their intellectual property and leverage its value in the market. This chapter delves into the intricacies of making the most of royalties and licensing, exploring the avenues that allow creators to monetize their creations and businesses to expand their reach.

Before delving into the strategies for maximizing these income streams, it is imperative to understand the basic concepts of royalties and licensing. Royalties are payments made to the intellectual property owner for using or selling that property. This can include patents, copyrights, trademarks, and other forms of intellectual assets. On the other hand, licensing involves granting permission to another party to use the intellectual property under specified conditions, often in
exchange for royalties.

Central to the discussion is the significance of intellectual property (IP). Intellectual property forms the foundation of many successful ventures, whether a groundbreaking invention, a bestselling novel, a chart-topping song, or a unique brand identity. Managing and exploiting these assets strategically can unlock new revenue streams and foster innovation.

One of the key strategies is to diversify the platforms through which your intellectual property is made available. This could involve licensing your music to multiple streaming services, publishing your book in various formats, or allowing different manufacturers to produce and sell your patented invention.

Expanding the geographical reach of your intellectual property through licensing agreements can significantly boost royalties. Licensing your product or content to international markets allows you to tap into diverse consumer bases and cultural landscapes.

Collaborating with other businesses through strategic partnerships can be a lucrative avenue. This could involve joint ventures, co-branding initiatives, or cross-licensing arrangements that mutually benefit all parties involved.

Embracing new technologies and adapting your intellectual property for emerging platforms is crucial. For example, exploring virtual reality, augmented reality, or incorporating artificial intelligence into your creations can open up novel revenue streams.

While royalties and licensing offer significant opportunities, they also come with challenges. These may include legal complexities, negotiating fair terms, and monitoring unauthorized use. The chapter will delve into these challenges and provide practical tips on navigating them effectively.

To illustrate the practical application of the strategies discussed, this chapter will include real-world case studies. These will showcase how individuals and businesses have successfully maximized their royalties and licensing income, offering valuable insights and inspiration for readers.

Making the most of royalties and licensing requires a strategic and adaptive approach. This chapter aims to equip creators and businesses with the knowledge and tools to successfully navigate the complexities of intellectual property monetization. By understanding the principles outlined here and applying them thoughtfully, individuals and enterprises can harness the full potential of their intellectual assets, driving both financial success and creative fulfillment.

Monetizing Your Intellectual Property

Intellectual property (IP) is a valuable asset that can be leveraged to generate income and contribute to the overall success of individuals, businesses, and organizations. This chapter will explore various strategies and methods for monetizing intellectual property, including patents, trademarks, copyrights, and trade secrets.

Before delving into monetization strategies, it's crucial to understand the different types of intellectual property clearly.

Patents protect inventions and innovations, granting the inventor exclusive rights for a specified period. Monetizing patents often involves licensing the technology to other companies or selling the patent outright.

Trademarks safeguard brand names, logos, and slogans, distinguishing products and services in the marketplace. Monetization can occur through licensing the trademark to third parties or selling merchandise featuring the trademark.

Copyrights protect original works of authorship, such as books, music, and software. Monetizing copyrights can involve licensing the content for various uses, such as reproduction, distribution, or public performance.

Trade secrets include confidential business information, such as formulas, processes, and customer lists. Monetizing trade secrets often involves entering into non-disclosure agreements (NDAs) and licensing the use of confidential information.

Licensing is a standard method of monetizing intellectual property. In a licensing agreement, the owner of the intellectual property grants another party the right to use, produce, or sell the protected material in exchange for royalty payments or other agreed-upon compensation.

Collaborating with other businesses through joint ventures can be a powerful strategy for monetizing intellectual property. This may involve combining complementary assets to create new products or services and sharing revenue among the partners.

For trademarks and copyrighted materials, merchandising can be a lucrative avenue for monetization. Licensing the use of a famous brand or character for merchandise such as clothing, accessories, or collectibles can generate substantial revenue.

In the digital age, subscription models have become increasingly popular for monetizing intellectual property. Content creators, software developers, and others can offer access to exclusive content or services through subscription-based platforms, generating recurring revenue.

Sometimes, outright selling or transferring intellectual property may be the most suitable option. This can involve selling patents, trademarks, copyrights, or trade secrets to interested buyers, providing a lump sum of capital.

While monetizing intellectual property can be rewarding, it comes with its own set of challenges and considerations. These may include legal complexities, market demand, competition, and the need for effective IP management strategies.

Monetizing intellectual property requires a strategic approach, considering the unique characteristics of each type of IP and the specific goals of the owner. Whether through licensing, joint ventures, merchandising, subscription models, or outright sales, a well-executed IP monetization strategy can unlock new revenue streams and enhance the overall value of intellectual assets. As the business landscape evolves, understanding how to monetize intellectual property effectively remains crucial for individuals and organizations.

Negotiating Profitable Licensing Deals

Negotiating profitable licensing deals is a delicate dance that requires strategic thinking, effective communication, and a thorough understanding of the market landscape. Whether you are a seasoned business professional or a budding entrepreneur, the ability to secure favorable licensing agreements can significantly impact the success and profitability of your venture. This chapter will explore critical strategies, tactics, and considerations to help you navigate the intricacies of negotiating licensing deals that benefit all parties involved.

Before entering into negotiations, it is crucial to have a clear understanding of your product or intellectual property's unique value proposition. Identify the key features, benefits, and differentiators that make your offering stand out. This knowledge will bolster your confidence during negotiations and serve as a foundation for articulating the value you bring to the table.

In-depth research is the cornerstone of successful negotiations. Gain a comprehensive understanding of the potential licensee's business, market positioning, and financial health. Thorough due diligence will empower you with valuable insights, allowing you to tailor your negotiation strategy to align with the specific needs and goals of the prospective partner.

Define your objectives and priorities before entering negotiations. Consider factors such as royalty rates, payment terms, exclusivity, and the duration of the licensing agreement. Establishing clear objectives provides a roadmap for negotiations and helps you maintain focus and avoid unnecessary concessions.

Negotiations are not just about numbers and terms but also about building relationships. Establishing trust with your potential licensee can pave the way for a more collaborative and mutually beneficial partnership. Foster open communication, actively listen to the other party's concerns, and demonstrate a commitment to finding solutions that meet both parties' needs.

Approach negotiations with a mindset of flexibility and creativity. While specific terms may be non-negotiable, be open to exploring alternative arrangements that can create value for both parties. Creative solutions often lead to win-win scenarios that enhance the overall success of the licensing deal.

Understand the leverage dynamics in play and leverage them to your advantage. Factors such as market demand, exclusivity, and the uniqueness of your offering can significantly impact your negotiating position. Additionally, timing is crucial; knowing industry trends and the competitive landscape can help you decide when to push for a deal.

Negotiating licensing deals can involve legal, financial, and strategic considerations. Seeking professional assistance, such as legal counsel or licensing experts, can provide valuable guidance and ensure the agreement is legally sound and aligned with your best interests.

Once negotiations reach a satisfactory point, ensure that all terms and conditions are clearly outlined in a written agreement. Attention to detail is paramount at this stage, as a well-drafted contract can prevent misunderstandings and disputes. Engage legal experts to review and finalize the agreement, providing an additional layer of assurance.

Negotiating profitable licensing deals requires preparation, strategic thinking, and effective communication. You can navigate negotiations successfully by understanding your value proposition, conducting thorough research, and building solid relationships. Stay flexible, be mindful of timing, and seek professional assistance to ensure the final agreement aligns with your business goals. Mastering the art of negotiating profitable licensing deals is a skill that can contribute significantly to your business's long-term success and sustainability.

Chapter 12: Navigating Tax Implications of Passive Income

In the intricate landscape of personal finance, pursuing passive income is a formidable strategy for wealth accumulation. As individuals strive to diversify their income streams and build a sustainable financial future, the allure of earnings without active day-to-day involvement becomes increasingly enticing. However, with this pursuit comes a crucial consideration that can significantly impact one's financial success – the taxation of passive income.

This chapter aims to guide you through the labyrinth of tax implications associated with passive income. Whether you are a seasoned investor, a budding entrepreneur, or someone exploring the possibilities of generating money while you sleep, understanding the tax landscape is paramount to optimizing your financial gains.

Before delving into the intricacies of taxation, let's take a moment to appreciate the evolution of passive income. Once confined to traditional investments such as dividends and interest, passive income has expanded its realms. Today, it includes revenue streams from real estate, peer-to-peer lending, royalties, and various digital assets. The expansive nature of passive income avenues has democratized wealth creation and presented a spectrum of tax implications.

Taxation is essential to any financial strategy, and passive income is no exception. The tax treatment of passive income is multifaceted, influenced by the type of income, jurisdiction, and the individual's overall financial situation. This chapter seeks to demystify taxation's complexity, clarifying how various passive income streams are taxed and strategies to optimize your tax liability legally.

Each passive income stream carries a unique set of tax considerations. From capital gains on investments to rental income from real estate, understanding the specific tax treatment for each type is crucial. We will explore how dividends, interest, capital gains, rental income, and other passive earnings are taxed, offering insights into tax-efficient strategies to preserve your hard-earned money.

Navigating the tax implications of passive income involves more than just understanding tax rates. It requires strategic thinking and leveraging tax-advantaged vehicles. We will explore how retirement accounts, tax-efficient investments, and other financial instruments can be utilized to minimize your tax burden and maximize the growth of your passive income portfolio.

Many individuals engage in passive income activities across borders in our interconnected world. International taxation adds complexity, whether you earn through foreign investments, digital products, or real estate in another country. This chapter will shed light on the tax implications of making passive income globally and guide navigating the global tax landscape.

Tax laws are dynamic, and compliance is non-negotiable. Adherence to tax regulations can lead to severe consequences. We will discuss the importance of accurate record-keeping, timely reporting, and compliance with tax laws to ensure a smooth and trouble-free journey in your passive income endeavors.

As you build your passive income empire, it's essential to consider the implications for your heirs. Proper estate planning can mitigate the tax burden on your successors and ensure the seamless transition of your wealth. This chapter will explore strategies for tax-efficient succession planning, safeguarding your legacy for future generations.

Embarking on the journey of passive income is a rewarding endeavor, but the seas are rife with challenges, especially regarding taxation. This chapter will equip you with the knowledge and tools to navigate these waters confidently. By the end, you'll understand the tax implications of your passive income and be empowered to make informed decisions that align with your financial goals.

So, let's set sail into passive income taxation, where informed choices become the wind in your financial sails.

Understanding Tax Efficiency

Tax efficiency is a crucial aspect of managing personal and business finances. It involves making strategic decisions to minimize the impact of taxes on your income, investments, and overall financial well-being. This chapter will delve into tax efficiency, explore various strategies to optimize your tax situation and provide practical insights for individuals and businesses.

Taxation is a significant expense that affects your financial growth and wealth accumulation. Understanding the importance of tax efficiency is the first step toward making informed financial decisions. Efficient tax planning can increase savings, improve investment returns, and enhance financial flexibility.

Before exploring tax efficiency strategies, one must grasp the different types of taxes individuals and businesses may encounter. These include income tax, capital gains tax, property tax, estate tax, and more. Each tax type has unique rules and implications; a comprehensive understanding of these is crucial for effective tax planning.

One of the primary areas where tax efficiency plays a significant role is in investments. Various investment vehicles come with different tax implications. Understanding how taxes apply to dividends, interest, and capital gains can help you design an investment portfolio that minimizes your tax burden. Tax-efficient investment strategies often involve utilizing tax-advantaged accounts, such as IRAs and 401(k)s, and considering tax-efficient investment vehicles like index funds.

Businesses also need to prioritize tax efficiency to optimize their profitability. Structuring a business tax-efficiently, taking advantage of available deductions, and understanding the tax implications of business transactions are crucial components of business tax planning.

Additionally, companies should explore tax credits and incentives offered by local and national governments to enhance tax efficiency further.

Tax-advantaged accounts, such as Health Savings Accounts (HSAs), 529 plans, and Roth IRAs, offer individuals unique opportunities to save money on taxes. Understanding the eligibility criteria, contribution limits, and tax benefits associated with these accounts allows individuals to decide where to allocate their resources for maximum tax efficiency.

Individuals must consider tax-efficient withdrawal strategies from their retirement accounts as they approach retirement. Proper planning can minimize taxes during retirement, ensuring that individuals can maximize their savings. Techniques such as Roth conversions, strategic Social Security claiming, and managing required minimum distributions (RMDs) are crucial in optimizing tax efficiency during retirement.

Tax laws and regulations are subject to change, and staying informed about these changes is essential for maintaining tax efficiency. Regularly reviewing your financial plan and adapting to new tax laws ensures that you optimize your tax situation over time.

Understanding tax efficiency is a continuous process that involves staying informed about tax laws, strategically planning investments, and making informed financial decisions. Incorporating tax efficiency into your financial strategy can enhance economic well-being, preserve wealth, and achieve long-term financial goals. A proactive and informed approach to tax efficiency is critical to financial success in the ever-evolving taxation landscape.

Strategies for Minimizing Tax Liabilities

Taxes are a significant aspect of personal and business finance. Understanding and implementing strategies to minimize tax liabilities is crucial for individuals and companies. This chapter explores various strategies that can be employed to optimize tax efficiency, reduce tax burdens, and ensure compliance with tax laws.

Effective tax planning is a year-round process, not just a last-minute scramble during tax season. By staying proactive and continually evaluating your financial situation, you can identify opportunities for tax savings. Regularly review your income, expenses, and investments to make informed decisions that align with your tax objectives.

Take advantage of tax-advantaged accounts to minimize your tax liabilities. Contributions to retirement accounts such as 401(k)s and IRAs can reduce your taxable income. Additionally, funds within these accounts can grow tax-deferred, providing an opportunity for compound growth.

Explore available tax credits and deductions to maximize your tax savings. Standard deductions include mortgage interest, medical expenses, and charitable contributions. Tax credits, such as the Child or Earned Income Tax Credit, directly reduce your tax liability and can result in significant savings.

Consider tax implications when making investment decisions. Long-term capital gains are typically taxed at a lower rate than short-term gains. Tax-loss harvesting can also be a valuable strategy for selling investments with losses to offset gains. Additionally, explore investments in tax-efficient funds that minimize distributions, reducing tax liability.

For businesses, effective tax planning involves careful consideration of business structures, expenses, and deductions. Selecting the proper legal structure, such as an LLC or S corporation, can have significant tax implications. Strategically managing business expenses and taking advantage of available deductions can reduce the overall tax burden.

Estate planning is about passing on wealth and minimizing the tax impact on your estate. Understand the current estate tax laws and consider using tools like trusts to protect assets and facilitate the smooth transfer of wealth. Gift-giving strategies can also be employed to reduce the size of your taxable estate.

For retirees, managing withdrawals from retirement accounts is crucial. Carefully plan the timing and amount of withdrawals to minimize the tax impact. Coordinating Social Security benefits and other income sources can help optimize your overall tax situation during retirement.
Tax laws are complex and subject to change. Stay informed about updates in tax regulations that may affect your financial situation. Consulting with a tax professional or financial advisor can provide

personalized guidance and help you navigate the ever-evolving tax landscape.

By incorporating these strategies into your financial planning, you can optimize your tax efficiency, preserve more of your hard-earned money, and ensure compliance with tax laws. Remember that tax planning is an ongoing process, and staying informed and seeking professional advice are essential components of a successful tax strategy.

Chapter 13: Building Multiple Streams of Passive Income

The quest for financial independence has taken on new dimensions. One of the critical strategies gaining momentum is building multiple streams of passive income. This approach offers financial security and opens doors to a lifestyle of freedom and flexibility. This chapter will delve into the fundamentals of building multiple passive income streams, exploring this financial strategy's what, why, and how.

Passive income is income earned with minimal effort or direct involvement. Unlike active income, where you exchange time and effort for money through traditional employment, passive income flows in even when you're not actively working. It's like a river that keeps flowing regardless of your presence.

Multiple streams of passive income involve creating diverse sources of revenue that collectively contribute to your financial well-being. These streams can take various forms, such as dividends from investments, rental income from real estate, royalties from intellectual property, and profits from online businesses. The beauty of this strategy lies in its ability to provide financial resilience by not relying on a single source of income.

Diversification is a cornerstone principle in finance, and it holds when building multiple passive income streams. Relying on a single income source exposes you to risks associated with that specific avenue. Economic downturns, market fluctuations, or industry-specific challenges can impact any singular source of passive income. By diversifying your income streams, you create a robust financial portfolio that can weather unforeseen challenges.

Diversifying your income streams provides a safety net. If one source is affected by external factors, the others can continue to generate income.

Passive income requires less active involvement; it allows you to pursue other interests, spend more time with family, or even explore new business ventures without jeopardizing your financial stability.

Multiple streams of passive income contribute to wealth accumulation over time. This wealth can be reinvested or utilized to create even more passive income, fostering a financial growth cycle.

Relying solely on a traditional job can be risky in today's dynamic job market. Building multiple passive income streams reduces your dependency on a single employer or industry.

Explore various investment opportunities like stocks, bonds, and real estate. Diversify your investment portfolio to mitigate risks.

Consider rental properties or real estate crowdfunding platforms to generate passive income through property ownership.

Leverage the power of the internet to create passive income streams through blogging, affiliate marketing, or creating and selling digital products.

If you possess skills or knowledge in a specific area, consider creating and licensing intellectual property, such as books, courses, or software.

Invest in dividend-paying stocks to receive regular payouts from successful companies.

While building multiple streams of passive income is appealing, it's essential to acknowledge the challenges involved. These may include initial time and financial investments, market volatility, and the need for ongoing management. However, these challenges can be overcome with strategic planning, persistence, and a willingness to learn.

We will explore each of the strategies mentioned above in greater detail, providing practical insights, case studies, and actionable steps to help you embark on your journey to financial independence through multiple streams of passive income. As we navigate through the intricacies of each avenue, you'll gain a comprehensive understanding of how to build, manage, and optimize diverse streams of income that align with your financial goals and lifestyle aspirations.

Diversifying Your Passive Income Portfolio

Building a diversified passive income portfolio is a crucial strategy. Diversification helps spread risk and enhances the resilience of your income streams. In this chapter, we'll explore the importance of diversification, various passive income sources, and practical tips for creating a well-rounded portfolio.

Diversifying your passive income portfolio is akin to putting only some of your eggs in one basket. The economic landscape is dynamic, and various factors can impact different income streams differently. Relying solely on one source of passive income exposes you to heightened risks. Diversifying can mitigate these risks and create a more robust financial foundation.

Risk is inherent in any investment or income-generating activity. Economic downturns, changes in consumer behavior, and shifts in market trends can affect the performance of individual assets. Diversification, however, helps offset the impact of poor-performing assets by including others that may respond differently to changing conditions.

The goal of diversification is not just risk mitigation but also the pursuit of stability. A mix of income streams can create a more consistent and reliable cash flow. This stability is especially crucial during economic uncertainties, as some income sources may remain resilient while others experience downturns.

Exploring a range of income sources is essential to diversify your passive income portfolio effectively. Here are some popular options:
Investing in dividend-paying stocks can provide a steady stream of income. Look for companies with a history of stable dividends and growth potential.

Real estate can offer both rental income and property value appreciation. Consider residential or commercial properties, real estate investment trusts (REITs), or crowdfunding platforms. Platforms facilitating peer-to-peer lending allow you to earn interest by lending money directly to individuals or small businesses.

Building and monetizing a website, blog, or online store can generate passive income through advertising, affiliate marketing, or product sales.
Create and sell digital products like e-books, online courses, or software. Once developed, these products can generate income with minimal ongoing effort.

Consider earning royalties from books, music, or art if you possess creative talents. Licensing your intellectual property can provide a steady income stream.

Utilize automated investment platforms and robo-advisors to build a diversified portfolio of stocks and bonds.

Before diversifying, assess your risk tolerance. Understand how comfortable you are with potential fluctuations in your income streams and adjust your portfolio accordingly.

Regularly research potential income sources and stay informed about market trends. This knowledge will help you make informed decisions and adapt your portfolio to changing conditions.

You can periodically review your passive income portfolio to ensure it aligns with your financial goals. Rebalance your investments if necessary, selling assets that may be overperforming and reinvesting in those with more growth potential.

Maintain an emergency fund to cover unexpected expenses. This provides a financial buffer, allowing you to navigate challenges without jeopardizing your income streams.

Diversification isn't just about investing in different asset classes; it's also about diversifying within those classes. For example, consider a mix of sectors and industries if you invest in stocks.

Diversifying your passive income portfolio is a strategic approach to building financial resilience. By incorporating various income sources, you can create a more robust portfolio and be better positioned to weather economic uncertainties. Please take the time to assess your goals, research potential income streams, and regularly review and adjust your portfolio to ensure it's continued. In doing so, you'll be on the path to creating a sustainable and diversified passive income stream.

Balancing Risk and Reward

The art of successful decision-making lies in the delicate dance between risk and reward. Life is a series of choices, and each choice carries with it a certain level of uncertainty. This chapter explores balancing risk and reward, understanding that every decision involves a trade-off between potential gains and losses.

Risk is an inherent aspect of any decision-making process. Whether in business, personal relationships, or everyday life, the potential for both positive and negative outcomes exists. Understanding the nature of risk is crucial to achieving a balanced approach.

You can begin by assessing the risks involved in a particular decision. What are the potential pitfalls, and what are the possible rewards? Evaluate the likelihood of various outcomes, considering both short-term and long-term consequences.

Please be aware that not all risks are quantifiable. Some uncertainties are inherently ambiguous, and the future is only partially predictable. Embrace the idea that ambiguity is part of the decision-making landscape and focus on managing it effectively.

While risk is the potential for loss, reward represents the potential for gain. Calculating the reward involves a thoughtful analysis of the benefits that may arise from a particular decision. Here are key considerations:
Could you clearly define what success looks like in the context of your decision? This could be financial gain, personal fulfillment, or achieving a specific goal. A clear definition of success helps assess whether the potential rewards align with your objectives.

Attempt to quantify the potential benefits associated with each decision. This could involve financial projections, personal growth metrics, or other relevant measures. By putting potential gains into tangible terms, you can better evaluate whether the rewards justify the inherent risks.
Balancing risk and reward requires strategic thinking and a nuanced approach. Consider the following strategies:

Diversifying your investments can help spread risk across different assets in financial decisions. Similarly, in life decisions, diversifying your experiences and skills can mitigate the impact of potential setbacks.

Please understand your risk tolerance. Everyone has a different comfort level when it comes to taking risks. Knowing your limits helps you make decisions that align with your personality and values.

Anticipate different scenarios and their potential outcomes. This involves considering best-case, worst-case, and most likely scenarios. By preparing for various possibilities, you can make more informed decisions.

Examining real-world examples of successful and unsuccessful decisions can provide valuable insights. By studying the experiences of others, you can gain a deeper understanding of the dynamics at play in balancing risk and reward.

Explore Apple's history, from the risk-taking decisions of launching innovative products to their calculated strategies in entering new markets. Apple's success demonstrates the importance of taking well-calculated risks in a rapidly changing environment.

The downfall of Enron serves as a cautionary tale about the dangers of unchecked risk-taking. Analyze the decisions and actions that led to the company's demise, highlighting the importance of ethical considerations in pursuing rewards.

Balancing risk and reward is an ongoing process that requires adaptability, resilience, and a willingness to learn from successes and failures. By cultivating a strategic mindset, understanding the nature of risk, and making informed decisions, you can navigate the complexities of life with a greater sense of balance and purpose.

Chapter 14: Overcoming Challenges on the Passive Income Journey

Embarking on the path to financial freedom through passive income is an exhilarating journey that promises independence, flexibility, and the potential for long-term wealth. However, like any worthy pursuit, the road to passive income has challenges. In this chapter, we will delve into the various obstacles that may arise on your passive income journey and explore practical strategies to overcome them.

One of the most common misconceptions about passive income is the belief in overnight success. Many aspiring entrepreneurs are lured by the promise of quick riches, only to discover that building sustainable passive income streams takes time, effort, and persistence. This section will explore the importance of realistic expectations and the mindset required to navigate the inevitable hurdles.

Investing, a key component of many passive income strategies, involves risk. Understanding and managing these risks is crucial for long-term success. This chapter will discuss various risks associated with passive income, from market fluctuations to unforeseen challenges, and offer guidance on risk mitigation strategies.

Creating passive income often requires an upfront investment of time, money, or both. Balancing these resources can be challenging, especially for individuals with existing commitments such as a full-time job or family responsibilities. We will explore practical tips on time management, prioritization, and finding the right balance to ensure progress without burnout.

The business landscape is dynamic, and what works today may be less effective tomorrow. Adapting to change is a fundamental skill on the passive income journey. This section will provide insights into staying agile, embracing innovation, and navigating the evolving landscape of passive income opportunities.

Patience is a virtue, but impatience can be a stumbling block in the fast-paced world of passive income. This chapter will address the challenges of waiting for returns to materialize, the importance of perseverance, and techniques to stay motivated during slow progress.

For many individuals, entering the realm of passive income may require acquiring new skills and knowledge. This section will explore the learning curve associated with different passive income streams, offering guidance on effective skill development and continuous learning.

The abundance of information in the digital age can lead to analysis paralysis, preventing individuals from taking action. We will discuss how to navigate the sea of information, make informed decisions, and avoid the trap of overthinking.

Overcoming challenges is often more manageable with a robust support system. This chapter will highlight the importance of building a network of mentors, peers, and like-minded individuals who can provide guidance, share experiences, and offer encouragement during the inevitable ups and downs.

In conclusion, while the path to passive income may present challenges, overcoming these obstacles separates the successful from the discouraged. This chapter aims to equip you with the mindset, strategies, and tools needed to navigate the challenges on your journey to financial freedom through passive income.

Common Pitfalls and How to Avoid Them

Success in any endeavor often hinges on navigating potential pitfalls and challenges. In pursuing your goals, you must be aware of common pitfalls and develop strategies to sidestep or overcome them. This chapter explores some prevalent stumbling blocks and offers insights on how to avoid them.

One of the most common pitfalls is a journey without a clear destination. Without well-defined goals and a strategic plan, individuals and organizations may be drifting aimlessly. To avoid this, please take the time to explain your objectives, create a roadmap, and periodically reassess and adjust your course as needed.

Procrastination can be a significant impediment to progress. Falling prey to the allure of instant gratification or delaying important tasks can hinder success. Combat procrastination by breaking tasks into smaller, manageable steps, prioritizing responsibilities, and adopting effective time management techniques.

Mistakes are inevitable, but failing to learn from them can be detrimental. Embrace mistakes as opportunities for growth and improvement. Analyze the reasons behind errors, make adjustments, and incorporate lessons learned into your future endeavors.

Taking risks is often necessary for progress, but doing so without careful consideration can lead to failure. Develop a risk management strategy that involves identifying potential risks, evaluating their impact, and formulating contingency plans. Balancing risk and reward is critical to avoiding catastrophic setbacks.

Communication breakdowns can derail even the most well-conceived plans. Whether in personal or professional settings, transparent and effective communication is essential. Foster open communication channels, actively listen to others, and provide feedback to ensure everyone is on the same page.

Burnout is a real threat when individuals neglect their well-being. To maintain sustained success, prioritize self-care. This includes adequate rest, regular exercise, and activities that bring joy. Recognize that a healthy mind and body are fundamental to long-term achievement.

In a rapidly evolving world, resistance to change can hinder progress. Embrace a growth mindset, be open to new ideas, and adapt to changing circumstances. Continuous learning and flexibility are crucial for staying relevant and thriving in dynamic environments.

Isolation can limit creativity and hinder problem-solving. Foster a collaborative mindset, both within and outside your immediate circles. Seek diverse perspectives, engage in constructive dialogue, and leverage the collective intelligence of a team.

Success is a journey, not just a destination. Refrain from acknowledging and celebrating small victories to avoid burnout and a lack of motivation. Take the time to recognize and appreciate progress, no matter how minor, to maintain a positive and motivated mindset.

Constructive feedback is a valuable tool for improvement. Ignoring or dismissing feedback can result in missed opportunities for growth. Please cultivate a receptivity to feedback, actively seek it out, and use it to refine your skills and approaches.

In conclusion, navigating the path to success requires vigilance and adaptability. Recognizing and actively addressing these common pitfalls can enhance your resilience and increase the likelihood of achieving your goals. Remember, each challenge presents an opportunity for growth and improvement.

Staying Resilient in the Face of Setbacks

Life is filled with peaks and valleys, successes and failures, triumphs and setbacks. No one is immune to facing challenges, and setbacks are an inevitable part of the human experience. The key to navigating these tumultuous waters lies in resilience—the ability to bounce back, learn from adversity, and emerge stronger than before.

Before delving into strategies for staying resilient, it's essential to recognize setbacks for what they are—a natural and often temporary part of life. Whether it's a professional setback, a personal disappointment, or a health challenge, setbacks are not an indication of failure but rather an opportunity for growth and self-discovery.

One of the cornerstones of resilience is adopting a growth mindset. Psychologist Carol Dweck coined this term to describe the belief that one's abilities and intelligence can be developed through dedication and hard work. Embracing a growth mindset allows individuals to view setbacks as learning, adapting, and improving opportunities. Instead of seeing failure as a dead-end, a person with a growth mindset sees it as a stepping stone to success.

In the face of setbacks, it's crucial to practice self-compassion. Treat yourself with the same kindness and understanding you would offer to a friend facing a similar situation. Acknowledge your emotions without judgment and recognize that setbacks are a universal human experience. Practicing self-compassion creates a supportive inner dialogue that helps you navigate challenges with greater resilience.

No one can go through life alone, especially during challenging times. Building a solid support system is a vital component of resilience. Surround yourself with friends, family, mentors, and colleagues who offer encouragement, understanding, and constructive feedback. A network of people who believe in your abilities and support your journey can provide the emotional sustenance needed to weather setbacks.

Sometimes, setbacks occur when our goals could be more realistic and ambitious. While it's essential to aim high, setting achievable and realistic goals is equally important. Break down larger goals into smaller, manageable tasks, and celebrate incremental successes. This approach makes setbacks less overwhelming and allows for a continuous sense of progress and accomplishment.

Every setback is an opportunity to learn and grow. Please take the time to reflect on the circumstances that led to the setback, identify areas for improvement, and then think about alternative strategies. Adversity can be an influential teacher, providing valuable insights and contributing to personal and professional development. Use setbacks as stepping stones to refine your skills, enhance your resilience, and build a more robust foundation for future success.

Resilience is closely tied to mental and emotional well-being. Mindfulness practices, such as meditation and deep breathing exercises, can help manage stress and foster a calm and focused mindset. By staying present at the moment, individuals can better navigate challenges, avoid unnecessary worry about the future, and maintain a clear perspective on their goals.

In the face of setbacks, it's easy to become fixated on the negative aspects of a situation. Counteract this tendency by celebrating small wins and achievements, no matter how minor they may seem. Recognizing and appreciating progress, no matter how incremental, fosters a positive mindset and reinforces the belief that setbacks are temporary obstacles to success.

Staying resilient in the face of setbacks is a lifelong journey that requires self-awareness, a growth mindset, and a supportive community. By understanding setbacks as opportunities for growth, practicing self-compassion, building a robust support system, setting realistic goals, learning from adversity, and incorporating mindfulness and stress management into daily life, individuals can navigate challenges with grace and emerge stronger on the other side. Remember, resilience is not the absence of adversity but the ability to thrive in its presence.

Chapter 15: Planning Your Exit Strategy

One of the most crucial yet often overlooked aspects is planning for the inevitable – the exit strategy. Whether you're a seasoned entrepreneur, a startup founder, or a business owner contemplating the next phase of your professional journey, understanding and strategically planning your exit is paramount. Chapter 15 is dedicated to unraveling the intricacies of "Planning Your Exit Strategy."

Exiting a business is a multifaceted process that demands careful consideration, meticulous planning, and a keen understanding of your personal and professional objectives. While it may seem counterintuitive to contemplate the end at the beginning, planning your exit is an integral part of the entrepreneurial journey. Whether you envision selling your business, passing it on to a successor, merging with another entity, or exploring alternative exit routes, a well-thought-out strategy is essential for maximizing value and ensuring a smooth transition.

The proactive consideration of an exit strategy is not an admission of defeat or an acknowledgment of a business's inevitable demise. Instead, it's a strategic move that empowers you to make informed decisions, capitalize on opportunities, and navigate potential challenges. By planning your exit, you gain the foresight to align your business goals with your aspirations and respond effectively to market dynamics.

Chapter 15 delves into the critical components of exit planning, offering insights into the following key areas:

1. Understanding Your Objectives:
   - Identifying personal and professional goals.
   - Defining financial expectations and lifestyle aspirations.

2. Valuation and Financial Readiness:

- Assessing the actual value of your business.
- Strengthening financial foundations for a robust exit.

3. Selecting the Right Exit Strategy:
   - Exploring options such as mergers and acquisitions, IPOs, family succession, or liquidation.
   - Evaluating the pros and cons of each strategy in the context of your business.

4. Building a Succession Plan:
   - Nurturing and preparing successors within the organization.
   - Ensuring a seamless transition of leadership.

5. Legal and Regulatory Considerations:
   - Understanding legal obligations and compliance.
   - Mitigating risks associated with the exit process.

Beyond the financial and logistical considerations, this chapter also addresses the emotional and psychological aspects of exit planning. It explores the impact on stakeholders, employees, and even the founder's sense of identity. Acknowledging and navigating these aspects is essential for a holistic and successful exit.

We embark on a journey to demystify the complexities surrounding exit planning. With knowledge, insights, and a strategic mindset, you can position yourself to exit your business successfully and leverage this transition as a springboard for new opportunities and personal fulfillment.

Join us as we navigate the intricate path of "Planning Your Exit Strategy."
Succession planning is a critical aspect of business strategy, especially for entrepreneurs and business owners looking to transition out of their roles and ensure the continued success of

their enterprises. Crafting a well-thought-out exit strategy requires careful consideration of various factors, including financial planning, leadership development, and stakeholder communication. This chapter will explore key strategies for effective business succession planning.

Successful business succession begins with early planning and a comprehensive assessment of the current state of the business. Owners should evaluate the company's financial health, identify key personnel, and assess potential successors. Early planning allows for identifying strengths and weaknesses within the organization, providing a solid foundation for strategic decision-making.

A crucial aspect of succession planning involves identifying and nurturing key talent within the organization. This may include grooming internal candidates for leadership roles or recruiting external candidates with the necessary skills and vision. Developing a leadership pipeline ensures a smooth transition and helps maintain continuity in the company's operations.

Clear and transparent communication is essential throughout the succession planning process. Owners must communicate their intentions and involve key stakeholders, including employees, customers, and suppliers. Transparent communication fosters trust and minimizes uncertainty, reducing potential disruptions during the transition.

Navigating the legal and financial aspects of succession planning is crucial. This includes estate planning, tax considerations, and the development of legal documents such as wills and buy-sell agreements. Engaging with legal and financial professionals early in the process can help ensure a seamless transition while minimizing tax implications.

Consideration should be given to the diversification of ownership, especially in family-owned businesses. Implementing structures such as trusts, holding companies, or employee stock ownership plans (ESOPs) can provide a mechanism for transferring ownership while preserving the company's values and culture.

Knowledge transfer is vital for a smooth transition. Owners should create a structured plan for transferring institutional knowledge to successors. This may involve mentorship programs, documentation of critical processes, and establishing a knowledge-sharing culture within the organization.

Unforeseen events can impact succession plans. Owners should develop contingency plans to address unexpected challenges, such as the sudden departure of a key executive or changes in market conditions. Contingency planning helps the business remain resilient in the face of uncertainty.

A gradual transition can be beneficial, allowing the outgoing owner to mentor the successor and ease them into their new role. This approach minimizes disruption and provides an opportunity for knowledge transfer and relationship building with key stakeholders.

After the transition, conducting a thorough evaluation of the succession process is essential. This includes assessing the performance of the new leadership, evaluating the impact on the business, and making adjustments as needed. Continuous improvement ensures the company's long-term success under new leadership.

Planning your exit strategy is a complex but necessary undertaking for business owners. By employing these strategies, you can enhance the likelihood of a successful transition, preserve the legacy of your business, and ensure its continued success in the hands of the next generation of leaders. Remember, effective succession planning is not just about leaving; it's about having a lasting and positive impact on the organization you've worked hard to build.

As you approach retirement, planning your exit strategy becomes crucial for ensuring a financially secure and fulfilling future. Your retirement years should be a time of relaxation, exploration, and enjoying the fruits of your labor. To make this possible, it's essential to carefully consider various aspects of your financial plan as you transition from the workforce to retirement.

Before delving into the specifics of your exit strategy, take the time to define your retirement goals. Consider both your short-term aspirations and long-term vision for this stage of life. Ask yourself questions such as:
1. Lifestyle: What kind of lifestyle do you envision during retirement? Do you plan to travel extensively, downsize your home, or engage in new hobbies?

2. Healthcare: Have you factored in potential healthcare expenses? How will you manage health insurance and unexpected medical costs?
3. Legacy: What legacy do you want to leave behind for your loved ones or charitable causes?

Understanding your retirement goals will guide your financial decisions and help you develop a tailored exit strategy.

Evaluate your current financial situation to determine whether you're prepared for retirement. Consider the following:

1. Retirement Savings: Review your retirement savings accounts, such as 401(k)s, IRAs, and pension plans. Could you assess whether your savings align with your retirement goals?

2. Social Security: Understand your Social Security benefits and the optimal time to start receiving them. Delaying benefits can lead to higher payouts.

3. Debt: Minimize outstanding debts before retirement to reduce financial stress. This includes mortgages, credit card debt, and any outstanding loans.

4. Emergency Fund: Maintain an emergency fund to cover unexpected expenses, ensuring you don't need to dip into your retirement savings prematurely.

Once you retire, your income stream will likely shift. Develop a withdrawal strategy to ensure your savings last throughout your retirement. Consider:

1. Budgeting: Develop a comprehensive budget that includes living expenses, healthcare costs, travel, and other discretionary spending.

2. Withdrawal Rate: Determine a sustainable withdrawal rate from your retirement savings. Financial advisors often suggest the 4% rule, withdrawing 4% of your savings annually, adjusted for inflation.

3. Tax Planning: Strategize your withdrawals to minimize tax implications. This may involve tapping into taxable, tax-deferred, and tax-free accounts strategically.

Shift your investment strategy to align with your retirement goals and risk tolerance. Consider:

1. Asset Allocation: Adjust your portfolio to prioritize income-generating investments and minimize exposure to high-risk assets.

2. Diversification: Maintain a diversified portfolio to spread risk across various asset classes.

3. Rebalancing: Regularly review and rebalance your portfolio to ensure it aligns with your risk tolerance and financial goals. Prepare for potential healthcare needs and consider your legacy through:

1. Long-Term Care Insurance: Evaluate the need for long-term care insurance to cover potential assisted living or nursing home expenses.
2. Estate Planning: Develop or update your estate plan, including wills, trusts, and beneficiaries.

3. Legacy Planning: Consider how you want to distribute your assets and ensure your loved ones know your wishes.

By addressing these critical components of your exit strategy, you can set the foundation for a secure and enjoyable retirement. I'd like you to regularly reassess your plan to adapt to changing circumstances and ensure your financial well-being throughout retirement. Consulting with a financial advisor can provide personalized guidance and expertise tailored to your situation.

The notion of legacy transcends the immediate success of a business. It involves the deliberate and thoughtful planning of an exit strategy that not only secures the financial future of the business owner but also ensures the continuity and prosperity of the enterprise. Crafting a lasting legacy is an art form that requires strategic foresight, meticulous planning, and a commitment to leaving behind a business that stands the test of time.

Exit planning is often an overlooked aspect of business strategy. Entrepreneurs may find themselves so engrossed in the day-to-day operations that they must remember the ultimate goal: creating a legacy.

Whether you plan to pass your business down to the next generation, sell it, or merge with another entity, an exit strategy is the compass that guides your journey and shapes the narrative of your business legacy.
Successful legacy building begins long before the actual exit. Ideally, the moment you embark on your entrepreneurial journey is the right time to start considering your exit strategy. This foresight allows you to make decisions today that will positively impact the future of your business.

You can begin by defining what legacy means to you. Is it about financial success, social impact, or a combination of both? Your exit strategy should align with your vision for the future of the business. This clarity will guide your decisions throughout the process.

A legacy lives on when the business is well-prepared for transition. This involves grooming the next generation of leaders, ensuring the organization has robust systems and processes, and fostering a culture of innovation and adaptability.

Transitioning your business to the next generation can be an advantageous and personal exit strategy. It requires identifying and nurturing individuals within the organization who have the potential to take the reins. Succession planning involves mentorship, training, and a gradual transfer of responsibilities.

If selling your business is the chosen path, increasing its market value is essential. This may involve optimizing operations, enhancing profitability, and building a solid brand. Engage with financial advisors, business brokers, and legal experts to navigate the complexities of a sale.

Joining forces with another entity can be a strategic move to secure the future of your business. This involves careful negotiations, due diligence, and a shared vision for the combined entity. Mergers and acquisitions can offer financial benefits and open up new growth opportunities.

A robust financial plan is the bedrock of a successful exit. Ensure your financial records are accurate and transparent. Address outstanding liabilities and optimize your business's financial health to maximize its value.

You can engage legal experts to navigate the legal landscape of your chosen exit strategy. This includes contracts, intellectual property rights, and compliance issues. Mitigating legal risks ensures a smooth transition and protects the legacy you've built.

Open and transparent communication is critical to successfully navigating an exit. Keep stakeholders, employees, and customers informed throughout the process. This builds trust and maintains the positive reputation of your business.

Exiting a business is not just a financial transaction; it's an emotional journey. Recognize and address the emotional toll it may take on you and your team. Celebrate the accomplishments, acknowledge the challenges, and communicate the positive impact your business has had on the lives of those involved.

Planning your exit strategy is not just a business transaction; it's a crucial step in creating a lasting legacy. It's about ensuring the business you've nurtured and grown continues to thrive beyond your tenure. By starting early, choosing the right exit strategy, mitigating risks, and addressing the emotional aspects, you can craft a legacy that endures—a legacy that transcends the balance sheet and becomes an integral part of the business narrative for generations to come. Remember, the legacy you leave is not just about what you did with your business; it's about what your business continues to do without you.

As you approach the pivotal stage of planning your exit strategy, it becomes crucial to consider your financial goals and how you can integrate charitable endeavors into this transition. Balancing personal and philanthropic objectives can lead to a more fulfilling exit strategy, allowing you to leave a lasting impact on your life and the broader community. This chapter explores the importance of aligning personal and charitable goals and offers guidance on striking the right balance.

A well-crafted exit strategy goes beyond financial considerations. It involves reflecting on your values, passions, and the legacy you want to leave behind. Integrating charitable goals into your exit plan allows you to contribute meaningfully to causes that matter to you, fostering a sense of purpose and fulfillment.

Consider the following questions as you navigate this intersection:
- What social or environmental issues are important to you?
- How can your wealth be a force for positive change?
- Are there specific charitable organizations or causes that resonate with your values?

Your exit strategy is an opportunity to create a lasting legacy beyond financial transactions. Philanthropy can be a powerful vehicle for channeling your resources toward meaningful causes. Whether you establish a charitable foundation, contribute to existing organizations, or initiate community projects, philanthropy allows you to impact the world positively.

Incorporate the following steps into your exit planning process: Please clearly explain the causes and issues that align with your values. This mission statement will guide your philanthropic efforts and ensure a focused and impactful approach.

You can explore the establishment of a charitable foundation or donor-advised fund. These structures provide flexibility and control over your philanthropic activities while offering potential tax benefits.

Please engage with philanthropic advisors who can help you navigate the complexities of charitable giving. They can assist in identifying impactful opportunities and ensuring your contributions align with your values.

While philanthropy adds a meaningful dimension to your exit strategy, it's essential to strike a balance that preserves your financial security. Consider the following tips:

Please look at your financial situation, accounting for personal expenses, lifestyle goals, and philanthropic commitments. This analysis will help you determine how much charitable giving can be integrated without jeopardizing your financial well-being.

Explore investment strategies that balance risk and return. Diversifying your portfolio can enhance financial resilience and stabilize personal and charitable goals.

Explore impact investing opportunities that align with your values. This approach allows you to generate financial returns while making a positive social or environmental impact.

Open communication is vital when integrating charitable goals into your exit strategy. Please talk about your intentions with family members, business partners, and key stakeholders to ensure they can get support for your philanthropic endeavors.

You can start discussions with your family about the values you wish to instill and the causes that matter to you. This can foster a shared sense of purpose and unity.

Communicate your charitable intentions with relevant stakeholders if your exit strategy involves a business transition. Transparency can build trust and help maintain the goodwill of your business network.

Recognize that philanthropy is dynamic and may evolve. You can periodically reassess your charitable goals, adjusting them to reflect changing priorities, emerging issues, or new opportunities for impact.
Consider the case of [Fictional Entrepreneur], who successfully integrated charitable goals into their exit strategy. By establishing a family foundation focused on education and community development, they secured their financial legacy and substantially impacted the lives of future generations.

Balancing personal and charitable goals in your exit strategy requires thoughtful consideration, strategic planning, and open communication. By aligning your financial success with meaningful contributions to society, you can create a legacy that extends far beyond the confines of your business. As you embark on this journey, remember that the most fulfilling exit is one that not only secures your future but also leaves a positive mark on the world.

Knowing When and How to Retire

As you journey through the various stages of life, the prospect of retirement looms as a significant milestone. Deciding when and how to retire is a complex and personal process that requires careful consideration of various factors. In this chapter, we will explore the key elements that can guide you in making informed decisions about your retirement.

One of the crucial aspects of retirement is ensuring you have the financial means to support your desired lifestyle. Start by evaluating your current financial situation, including savings, investments, and debts. Engage with a financial advisor to create a comprehensive retirement plan that aligns with your goals and risk tolerance.

Consider your anticipated expenses in retirement, including healthcare, housing, and leisure activities. Understanding your spending patterns will help you determine the income required to maintain a comfortable lifestyle during retirement.

Explore the potential benefits available through Social Security and any employer-sponsored pension plans. Understanding how these income streams integrate into your overall financial plan is essential for making informed decisions about when to retire.

Retirement is not just a financial decision; it's also about finding purpose and fulfillment in this new phase of life. Consider your passions, hobbies, and interests, and explore how to incorporate them into your retirement years.

Assess your current health and consider potential healthcare needs in retirement. Understand the implications of healthcare costs and how they may impact your financial plan. Prioritize maintaining a healthy lifestyle to enhance your overall well-being during retirement.

Retirement often involves a significant shift in daily interactions. Consider how you will maintain social connections and relationships outside of the workplace. Engaging in community activities, joining clubs, or volunteering can contribute to a fulfilling retirement.

Determining the optimal time to retire involves balancing financial readiness with personal aspirations. You can assess your emotional and physical preparedness and financial stability to identify the ideal retirement window.

Explore the possibility of a phased retirement, where you gradually reduce your working hours before fully retiring. This approach can provide a smoother transition, allowing you to test the waters of retirement while maintaining some income level.

Please consult with legal and tax professionals to understand the implications of retirement on your estate, taxes, and any legal obligations. Proper planning can minimize tax liabilities and ensure a smooth transition of assets.

Retirement planning is an ongoing process. Regularly review your financial plan, reassess your goals, and adjust your strategies as needed. Economic conditions, health, and personal circumstances may change, necessitating adjustments to your retirement plan. After retiring, continue to engage in activities that bring joy and purpose. Consider pursuing new interests, traveling, or contributing to community projects. Staying active and involved can positively impact your overall well-being.

Knowing when and how to retire involves a careful blend of financial planning, emotional considerations, and lifestyle choices. By thoroughly assessing your financial readiness, emotional preparedness, and personal aspirations, you can make informed decisions that lead to a fulfilling and secure retirement. Please regularly revisit and adjust your retirement plan to ensure a smooth and enjoyable transition into this next chapter of your life.

Securing a Lasting Legacy

The desire to leave a lasting legacy is a common thread that transcends generations. It is the yearning to be remembered not just for what we have accomplished during our time on this earth but for our positive impact on others and the world around us. Creating a lasting legacy requires intentional thought, careful planning, and a commitment to values beyond one's existence.

Before embarking on the journey to secure a lasting legacy, it's crucial to reflect on what you want that legacy to be. Consider the values, principles, and beliefs that define you. Ask yourself what mark you want to leave on the world and how you want to be remembered by those whose lives you've touched.

Define the core values and principles that guide your life. These are the foundation upon which your legacy will be built. Whether it's integrity, compassion, innovation, or social justice, identifying these values will help shape the impact you want to make.

Consider the impact you want to have on the lives of others. This could be through mentorship, philanthropy, education, or any other avenue that aligns with your values. Think about how you can contribute to the betterment of society and the well-being of those who come after you.
Once you have a clear vision of your legacy, the next step is to translate that vision into a tangible plan. Legacy planning involves a strategic approach to ensure that your values endure and your impact is sustained.

Work with legal and financial professionals to create a comprehensive estate plan. This includes drafting a will, establishing trusts, and making provisions to distribute your assets. Could you allocate resources to causes and organizations that reflect your values?

You can explore philanthropic opportunities that align with your values. Whether through a family foundation, charitable trusts, or direct donations, philanthropy can be a powerful tool for creating a positive and lasting impact on the causes you care about.

Consider creating a written or recorded document that encapsulates your life lessons, experiences, and wisdom. This can be a valuable resource for future generations, providing insights into your values, decision-making processes, and the lessons you've learned.

A lasting legacy is not just about what you leave behind; it's also about the relationships you build and nurture throughout your life. Take an active role in mentoring others. Please share your knowledge, experiences, and insights with those who can benefit from them.

Mentorship is a powerful way to ensure that your legacy lives on through the growth and success of others.

Strengthen your bonds with family and community. Actively participate in the lives of your loved ones and contribute to the well-being of your community. Your positive influence within these circles will contribute significantly to the legacy you leave behind.

A lasting legacy is not a static entity; it evolves. Embrace a mindset of continuous growth and adaptation to ensure your legacy remains relevant and impactful.

Stay curious and open to learning. Embrace innovation and change, adapting to new ideas and technologies. A legacy that endures can adapt to the evolving needs of society.

Consider the environmental impact of your actions and your legacy on the planet. Sustainable practices and a commitment to environmental stewardship can be integral components of a legacy that values the well-being of future generations.

Securing a lasting legacy is a profound and meaningful endeavor. It requires a thoughtful and intentional approach to defining values, planning for the future, cultivating relationships, and embracing growth. Investing time and energy into these areas ensures your legacy is enduring and positively shaping the world for future generations.

Conclusion

As we reach the final pages of "The Passive Income Playbook: Building Wealth While You Sleep," we must reflect on our journey together. The principles and strategies shared throughout this book were designed to impart knowledge and inspire action. As you close this chapter, please carry the essence of passive income into the future.

Take a moment to acknowledge the progress you've made. Whether you're just starting your passive income journey or have already seen significant results, every step is a victory. Celebrate the small wins, learn from the setbacks, and understand that building wealth while you sleep is a continuous process.

We've explored the diverse passive income avenues, from real estate investments to online businesses and dividend stocks. The power of diversification has been a recurring theme, emphasizing the importance of creating multiple streams of passive income. Remember, the landscape of wealth creation is ever-evolving, and your ability to adapt is a crucial determinant of success.

Beyond the financial strategies, cultivating a wealth mindset is paramount. The ability to think long-term, embrace risk intelligently, and stay disciplined in the face of challenges will serve you well on your passive income journey. As you encounter obstacles, view them as opportunities for growth and learning rather than roadblocks.

True wealth goes beyond financial abundance; it encompasses our impact on the world. Consider how your passive income endeavors can contribute to the well-being of others. Whether through charitable giving, mentorship, or supporting causes close to your heart, the joy of wealth amplifies when shared.

"The Passive Income Playbook" isn't just a guide; it's an invitation to a lifestyle. As you continue, remember that the destination is not a singular point but a continual evolution. Keep refining your strategies, exploring new opportunities, and staying attuned to the ever-changing landscape of passive income.

The pages of this book may be coming to a close, but your journey toward financial freedom is just beginning. With the knowledge, mindset, and strategies outlined in these chapters, you have the tools to build wealth while sleeping. Take the reins of your financial destiny, and may your next chapter be filled with prosperity, growth, and the fulfillment of your dreams.

Thank you for joining me on this exploration of passive income. Here's to the exciting chapters ahead and the wealth you will continue to build, even as you sleep.

Wishing you abundance and success,
CHARLIE DALLAS
Author, "The Passive Income Playbook"

APPENDIX

Congratulations on reaching the appendix of "The Passive Income Playbook: Building Wealth While You Sleep." This section is your gateway to a wealth of online tools and platforms that can empower your passive income endeavors. Below, you'll find a carefully curated list of websites and apps to help you navigate the intricate landscape of financial freedom.

1. Investing Platforms:
   - Robinhood (https://robinhood.com/): A user-friendly platform for stock and ETF investing, offering commission-free trades.
   - RealtyMogul (https://www.realtymogul.com/): A real estate crowdfunding platform catering to both accredited and non-accredited investors.

2. Financial Education:
   -Investopedia (https://www.investopedia.com/): A comprehensive resource for financial education, featuring articles, tutorials, and tools.
   - Khan Academy - Finance (https://www.khanacademy.org/college-careers-more/personal-finance): Free educational content covering a wide range of financial topics.

3. Passive Income Communities:
   -BiggerPockets (https://www.biggerpockets.com/): Connect with real estate investors, access valuable resources, and learn from experienced professionals.
   - Reddit - Passive Income Subreddit (https://www.reddit.com/r/passive_income/): Engage with a community of individuals sharing insights and experiences in generating passive income.

Apps:

1. Personal Finance:
   - Mint (https://www.mint.com/): A popular app for budgeting, tracking expenses, and setting financial goals.
   - YNAB (You Need A Budget) (https://www.youneedabudget.com/): Focuses on helping users allocate every dollar to maximize financial control.

2. Investment and Retirement Planning:
   - Acorns (https://www.acorns.com/): Invest spare change automatically and grow your wealth over time.
   - Vanguard (https://investor.vanguard.com/home/): A well-known investment platform offering retirement planning tools and resources.

3. Real Estate:
   - Zillow (https://www.zillow.com/): Explore real estate listings, estimate property values, and research housing markets.
   - Airbnb (https://www.airbnb.com/): If you're considering short-term rentals, Airbnb is a popular platform for listing and managing properties.

4. Cryptocurrency:
   - Coinbase (https://www.coinbase.com/): A user-friendly platform for buying, selling, and managing various cryptocurrencies.

5. Freelancing and Online Businesses:
   - Upwork (https://www.upwork.com/): Connect with freelancers or offer your services to a global marketplace.
   - Shopify (https://www.shopify.com/): Build and manage your online store, exploring the world of e-commerce.

6. Tax and Legal:

- LegalZoom (https://www.legalzoom.com/): Obtain legal services and documentation for your business and investment ventures.

- TurboTax (https://turbotax.intuit.com/): A popular platform for filing taxes and staying compliant with the latest tax laws.